A NEW OWNER'S
GUIDE TO
BICHONS FRISES

JG-130

The Publisher wishes to acknowledge the following owners of the dogs in this book: Gail Antetomaso, Rick Beauchamp, Karen A. Chesbro, Jill Cohen, Bill Dreker, Florence Erwin, Annette Feldblum, Toby Frisch, Sherry Fry, Pam Goldman, Eleanor Grassick, A. Haarlem, George and Nancy Harrell, Judith Hilmer, Gail Huston, J. Kauppinen, Estelle and Wendy Kellerman, Robert Koeppel, Lori Kornfeld, Maurice and Florence Lillien, Gene and Mary Ellen Mills, Lois Morrow, Jerome Podell, Nancy Shapland, Barbara Stubbs, Frank Vallely, Caroline and Richard Vida, Rudy Van Woorst, Pauline Waterman.

Photographers: John L. Ashbey, Rick Beauchamp, Tara Darling, Anthony Delprete, Bill Dreker, Isabelle Francais, Sara Nugent, Alice Pantfoeder, Robert Pearcy, Sally Richerson, Vince Serbin, Missy Yuhl.

The author acknowledges the contribution of Judy Iby of the following chapters: Sport of Purebred Dogs, Identification and Finding the Lost Dog, Traveling with Your Dog, Health Care, Behavior and Canine Communication.

The portrayal of canine pet products in this book is for general instructive value only; the appearance of such products does not necessarily constitute an endorsement by the authors, the publisher, or the owners of the dogs portrayed in this book.

T.F.H. Publications, Inc.
One TFH Plaza
Third and Union Avenues
Neptune City, NJ 07753

This book has been published with the intent to provide accurate and authoritative information in regard to the subject matter within. While every precaution has been taken in preparation of this book, the publisher and author assume no responsibility for errors or omissions. Neither is any liability assumed for damages resulting from the use of the information herein.

ISBN 0-7938-2779-5

www.tfh.com

A New Owner's Guide to
BICHONS FRISES

Andrew "Gene" and
Mary Ellen Mills

Contents

The Bichon's curious nature is evident from a young age.

The Bichon's "powder puff" coat gives him a distinctive look.

Playful Bichons have all kinds of friends!

Bichon puppies are just full of affection.

The highly trainable Bichon is much more than a lap dog.

DEDICATION

To our many friends and breeders of the Bichon Frise who have dedicated themselves to the protection and betterment of the breed. A special thanks to Richard G. Beauchamp, who has so generously shared his knowledge and friendship, and to Ginger Crane Le Cave, who quietly stepped in to help when it was needed most.

Ch. Cali-Col Villanelle, the authors' first champion Bichon Frise and the foundation of their Drewlaine Kennel.

Multiple Best of Breed and Group winner Ch. Drewlaine Beau Monde Batiste and her handler, Michael Kemp. Bred by Nancy Shapland, Gene and Mary Ellen Mills and Richard G. Beauchamp.

HISTORY of the Bichon Frise

s is the case with so many of today's breeds of dog, the actual origin of the Bichon Frise (pronounced Bee-shawn Free-say, plural Bee-shawns Free-says) is clouded in obscurity. What is accepted as certainty is that the breed is descended from very small, frequently white lap dogs. These little dogs were the treasured pets of ladies who resided throughout the Mediterranean area as early as 600–300 BC. It is said that several known breeds descended from this root stock: the original Toy Poodle, the Maltese, and four types or sub-groups of the Bichon.

At some point during that same time period it appears that the ladies' little lap dogs were crossed with the Barbet, a spaniel-type dog known to exist then as well. The result was a group of dogs that came to be known as Barbichons. The name of that family was later shortened to Bichon. Because of their sturdy constitution, small size, and charming personalities, Bichons became very popular household companions. The Bichon family was later to evolve into four distinct breeds: the Bichon Maltaise,

The Maltese, along with the Bichon, descended from the small, mostly white dogs that were the treasured pets of ladies in the Mediterranean region as early as 600—300 BC.

The Bichon Frise's small size and delicate beauty made him a trendy and fashionable pet during the Renaissance years in Europe.

the Bichon Havanais, the Bichon Bolognaise, and our Bichon Frise. Their story is a fascinating one.

As land and sea trade flourished throughout Europe, some of the world-traveling tradesmen and sailors took their little Bichon companions with them. The company of the little dogs eased the loneliness of journeys that often meant being away from home for several years. The dogs captured the fancy of people in foreign lands and soon became coveted gifts or items of trade.

It is difficult, if not impossible, to know what other breeds were blended into the existing bloodlines of the little exported Bichons, but distinct characteristics began to differentiate the Bichons in different countries. One of these subgroups was known to have developed on the isle of Malta in the Mediterranean Sea. It was known as the Bichon Maltaise. No one knows for sure if these dogs were the forerunners of the modern Maltese, but those who ascribe to this theory do have plausible reason for doing so. A reoccurring fault in the Maltese

This white Havanese resembles his "cousins," but unlike the Bichon Frise and the Maltese, the Havanese can be seen in a variety of colors other than white.

of today is a woolly stand-off type coat, which is typical of the correct coat of the Bichon family.

Still other members of the Bichon family accompanied Spanish seamen on their voyages. At the high point of developing trade routes throughout the world, Spain's trading vessels reached the Americas and the island of Cuba. It appears that the Bichon was exceptionally popular, particularly in Havana, and after taking up residence there developed into that branch of the family known as the Havana Silk Dog or Bichon Havanais.

The Havanese is the smallest member of the Bichon family and weighs an average of 8 to 12 pounds. Unlike its other all-white cousins, the Bichon Havanais comes in all colors.

Italy also embraced the Bichon, and the breed became very popular, particularly in and around the city of Bologna. There the breed was held in very high regard and could often be seen accompanying the members of the royal family.

Visiting dignitaries from France and Spain were charmed by the little dogs and when these visitors returned home from Italy they were often given "Bichons Bolognaise" as gifts. Thus, the Bichons became status symbols in many parts of Europe. Today the physical appearance of the Bichon Bolognaise most closely resembles that of its cousin, the Bichon Frise. Probably the greatest difference between the two breeds is in the more reserved attitude of the Bolognaise. The Bolognaise is not quite as outgoing a breed as the Bichon Frise.

It seems almost certain that the same Spanish tradesmen who carried the Bichon to Cuba took still others of the breed to the many islands throughout the Atlantic, including Tenerife and the Canaries. Again, it is only conjecture to imagine what other breeds came into the Bichon picture while the breed propagated there, but, regardless, the breed did remain and it flourished. Eventually the breed was to come full circle, returning as a curiosity to both Spain and Italy. When it returned, however, it was known as the Bichon Tenerife—a name it would carry for several centuries.

In the 1500s, the Bichon Frise, then known as the Bichon Tenerife, was very popular with royalty and high society.

Ch. Devon Puff and Stuff demonstrates the playful demeanor that made the Bichon Frise a popular street performer.

During the 1500s, the French were highly influenced by Italy's Renaissance and it was very fashionable in France to adopt everything Italian. Part of the fashion trend in the French Courts was Italy's little white Bichon Tenerife. Francis I, patron of the Renaissance (1515–1547 AD), was particularly fond of the breed during his reign.

Little appears in French literature about the Tenerife dog after that period until the rise of Napoleon III into power in the early years of the 19th century. The Bichon Teneriffe is frequently mentioned in French literature during that

Bichons have the unique ability to walk on their hind legs. Many owners are amazed at how quickly their dogs take to performing this trick.

century and is frequently portrayed with members of the royal court in the works of leading artists of the period.

By the end of the 19th century, the breed was no longer favored by the royal court. However, hardy breed that it was, the Bichon Tenerife survived and was often found in the streets of Paris and other cities accompanying tradesmen and street musicians. The nimble Bichons were highly trainable and loved to perform for the crowds. The breed demonstrated a unique ability to walk on its hind legs for long distances and usually did so while pawing the air, which passers-by interpreted as begging for money. Of course, they good-humoredly contributed.

Europe's great circuses and carnivals took advantage of the Bichon's extroverted personality and uncanny ability to learn and perform tricks. The dogs were undoubtedly bred and the offspring selected with the ability to entertain in mind. To this day, the breed retains its entertaining capabilities and Bichon owners are amazed to find their dogs walking on their hind legs, performing somersaults, and performing feats of dexterity with no training whatsoever.

Were it not for the indestructible constitution of the Bichon, the breed could well have been lost to us during World Wars I and II.

Reduced to minimal numbers by the end of World War I, the breed escaped extinction only through the efforts of a few valiant fanciers who gathered what remained of the breed. They adopted an official breed standard under the auspices of the Societé Centrale Canine in March of 1933. The breed was officially given the name "Bichon à Poil Frisé" which, translated into English, means "Bichon of the curly hair."

Just when it looked as though devotees had secured the future of the Bichon Frise, another great war threatened the newly named breed. Here again, the breed's hardiness and the owners' determination assisted the Bichon Frise through this next devastating ordeal.

In the early 1950s, Helen and François Picault became actively interested in the Bichon. The couple lived in Dieppe, France, located on the English Channel just north of Paris. Their first Bichon so delighted them that they decided to begin a breeding program. They purchased Étoile and Eddy White de Steren Vor from Madame Abadie, owner of the leading Bichon Frise kennel in France. The Picaults began to breed and show

Bichons are popular pets around the world. This Bichon is pictured on the front porch of his home in Paris.

An important trio of Bichons: Ch. Cali Col's Robspierre, Ch. Reenroy's Ami du Kilkanny and Petit Gallant de St. George.

their own dogs, often journeying to the important events held in and around Paris.

Encouraged by the success of their dogs in France, the Picaults felt that this was a breed that would find interest among Americans as well. Accompanied by their three original Bichons, four additional females, and the newly registered kennel prefix "de Hoop," the Picaults set sail for America. They arrived in the United States in October of 1956 with what was to become the foundation stock of the Bichon Frise in America.

The Picaults settled briefly in Milwaukee but, to their dismay, found only little interest in the breed among dog fanciers there. Further, there were restrictions that prohibited their non-recognized breed from entering the hallowed halls of American Kennel Club dog shows.

In hopes of attracting attention and interest in the breed, the Picaults stationed themselves outside dog show venues and had their Bichon family put on shows not unlike those staged by the vendors and organ grinders of days gone by in Europe. Still, there was little recognition of their efforts. This, combined with the sub-zero temperatures of Wisconsin's winters, made the Picaults opt for yet another move, this time to the more hospitable climate of southern California.

California was no more accepting of this nondescript-appearing French breed than the dog fancy in Wisconsin—until a chance meeting with a Collie breeder, Gertrude Fournier. Mrs. Fournier found the little dogs charming and decided to assist the Picaults in their efforts to find acceptance for the breed.

Soon Mrs. Fournier was involved in a full-scale breeding operation under her Cali-Col kennel prefix. However, there was still little movement toward acceptance of the breed in the United States other than with those who had already been seduced by the charms of the Bichon. In spite of complete lack of interest among American dog fanciers, those dedicated to the little white immigrants banded together and formed the Bichon Frise Club of America in May of 1964.

But it was fate that was to step into the picture and send the breed skyrocketing to fame and fortune not only in America but also throughout the world. Barbara Stubbs, a resident of La Jolla, California, had acquired two Bichons and became so enthused with

Thelma Brown judged a large entry at the Bichon Frise Club of America's 1969 National Specialty. This event took place before AKC breed recognition.

16

The late Eve Arden and actress Betty White with a group of Bichons on Pet Set, a TV show of the late 1960s.

their trainability and amiable temperaments that she decided to assist the small band of fanciers who championed the cause of the breed. She, along with several founding members of the Bichon Frise Club of America, began to work in earnest on behalf of the breed.

It was Mrs. Stubbs who formulated a plan for advancing the cause of the breed, and she began her campaign by soliciting the help of two dog fanciers prominent on the all-breed scene at that time: Richard Beauchamp, then editor and publisher of the all-breed dog magazine *Kennel Review*, and Frank T. Sabella, who was at that time one of the leading professional dog handlers.

The combined efforts of the two gentlemen and the subsequent publicity obtained through *Kennel Review* "legitimatized" the breed in the minds of American dog fanciers. Within just a few years, the breed went from total obscurity to full recognition by the American Kennel Club. In April 1973, the AKC gave the Bichon full breed status as a participant in the Non-Sporting Group. The Bichon Frise Club of America sponsored a gala weekend in Las Vegas, Nevada, to mark the breed's first AKC show and, from that point on, it seemed as if there was no stopping the breed in its rise to popularity.

By this time, Barbara Stubbs had added another Bichon to her original pair, thus creating the trio that was to have a profound

Ch. Drewlaine Eau de Love, owned by the authors, was sired by Ch. Chaminade Mr. Beau Monde out of Ch. Cali-Col's Villanelle.

effect upon the breed. From these three Bichons, in combination with other major bloodlines, descended the pillars of the breed: the top-producing sire of all time, Ch. Chaminade Mr. Beau Monde; the top-producing dam of all time, Ch. Beau Monde The Fire Cracker; the top-winning Bichon of all time, Ch. Devon Puff and Stuff; and the breed's first all-breed Best in Show winner, Ch. Chaminade Syncopation.

Major accomplishments were to come fast and furious. Only a few months after the Bichon's entry into AKC competition, the first all-breed Best in Show win for the breed in America took place at the Framington Valley Kennel Club. The win was taken by Mrs. William Tabler's Ch. Chaminade Syncopation, who was known as "Snidely Whiplash" by his many friends and the new friends he made for the breed. Snidely was bred by Barbara Stubbs and Richard Beauchamp.

Many top awards were to follow for Snidely and other members of the breed in ensuing years. As popularity increased in the United States, the breed created interest internationally and many American-bred Bichons traveled to foreign countries where they were equally well received.

Without a doubt, one of the breed's most famous individuals was Nancy Shapland's homebred Ch. Devon Puff and Stuff. "Puff" cut a huge swath of wins throughout America and became the top winner of all time. It was her sparkling personality more than her winning ways that captured the heart of America. Puff was handled by professional handler Michael Kemp, who was nationally respected for his expertise in the ring.

Puff, however, cared little for Kemp's training or his reputation and more than once escaped her show lead and led her handler on a merry chase around the ring. One such occasion occurred in February of 1985 on the night of her Non-Sporting Group win at New York's Madison Square Garden, which is the venue for the nationally televised Westminster Kennel Club dog show. The televised escapade endeared the mischievous extrovert to audiences throughout America and turned the little street dog of France into a free-spirited international celebrity.

CHARACTERISTICS of the Bichon

Before anyone tries to decide whether the Bichon Frise is the correct breed for them, a larger, more important, question must be asked. That question is, "Should I own a dog at all?" Dog ownership is a serious and time-consuming responsibility that should not be entered into lightly. Failure to understand this can make what should be a rewarding relationship one of sheer drudgery. It is also one of the primary reasons for thousands upon thousands of unwanted dogs ending their lives in the gas chambers of humane societies and animal shelters throughout America.

If the prospective dog owner lives alone, all he needs do is be sure that he has a strong desire to make the necessary commitment that dog ownership entails. In the case of a family household, it is vital that the person who will ultimately be responsible for the dog's care really wants a dog. In the average household, the mother is most often given the additional responsibility of caring for the family pets. Children are away at school all day and the father is at work, and often it is the mother who is saddled with the additional chores of housebreaking, feeding, and trips to the veterinarian with what was supposed to be a family project.

Nearly all children love puppies and dogs and will promise anything to get one. But childhood enthusiasm can wane very quickly and it will be up to the adults in the family to ensure that the dog receives proper care. Children should be taught responsibility, but to expect a living, breathing, and needy animal to teach a child this lesson is incredibly indifferent to the needs of the animal.

There are many households in which the entire family is gone from early morning until late in the day. The question that must be asked is, "Who will provide food for the dog and access to the out-of-doors so that the dog can relieve itself?" This is something that can probably be worked out with an adult dog, but it is totally unfair for anyone to expect a young puppy to survive these conditions.

Should an individual or family find that they are capable of providing the proper home for a dog or young puppy, suitability of breed must also be considered. Here it might be worthwhile to look at the difference between owning a purebred dog and one of mixed ancestry. A mongrel can give you as much love and devotion as a purebred dog. However, the manner in which the dog does this and how its personality, energy level, and the amount of care it requires suit an individual's lifestyle are major considerations. In a purebred dog, most of these considerations are predictable to a marked degree even if the dog is purchased as a very young puppy. A puppy of uncertain parentage will not give you this assurance.

All puppies are cute and fairly manageable, but someone who lives in a two-room apartment will find life difficult with a dog that grows to the size of a Great Dane. The mountain climber or

"Will you take good care of me?" Murray asks his owners with the inquisitive expression that is typical of the Bichon.

marathon runner is not going to be happy with a short-nosed breed that has difficulty catching its breath simply walking across the street on a hot day.

An owner who expects his dog to sit quietly by his side while he watches television or reads is not going to be particularly happy with a high-strung off-the-wall dog whose rest requirements are 30 seconds out of every ten hours. Nor is the outdoorsman going to be particularly happy with a long-coated breed that attracts every burr, leaf, and insect in all of nature. Knowing what kind of dog best suits your lifestyle is not just a consideration, it is paramount to the foundation of your life-long relationship with the dog.

LIFE WITH A BICHON

All of the foregoing applies to whether or not you should own a Bichon Frise. Further, as greeting-card appealing as a Bichon puppy might be, you must remember that it is a white dog that needs frequent bathing in order to stay white. It should also be understood that the Bichon is the eternal child and enjoys playing in the mud or burying himself in the sandbox as much as any human child would.

The Bichon is a long-coated breed that will only stay looking like a Bichon as long as you are willing to keep him brushed and either

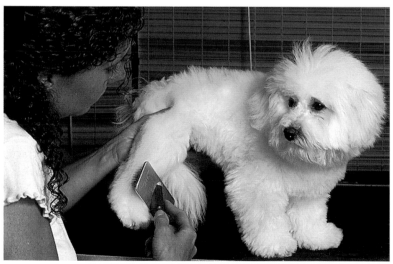

The Bichon's long, white, double coat will only stay clean and mat-free if you are willing to invest some time and effort into his grooming.

Despite its small size, the Bichon is hardy enough to run with the "big dogs." Emily plays with her Rottweiler friend Allegra.

learn to trim his coat yourself or spend the necessary money to have it done professionally. If you appreciate the look of the breed, you should realize that it will take some time and effort on your part to keep your Bichon looking that way.

While the Bichon Frise can be an ideal choice for the person with allergy problems, it must be remembered that the breed, like many all-white and pink-skinned dogs, can be extremely sensitive to fleas. Unless carefully controlled, flea bites can and will lead to severe scratching that results in skin eruptions and "hot spots" that are accompanied by hair loss.

If you are willing to make the necessary commitment that a Bichon requires, let us assure you that there are few breeds that are any more versatile, amiable, and adaptable. Don't overlook the breed's history. Bichons have been pampered pets of the nobility, seafarers, street urchins, and circus entertainers, as well as a practically endangered species. With a history of this kind, it should go without saying that they can fit into most any caring household.

The breed is hardy and not prone to chronic illnesses. The Bichon is of a handy size—neither so large as to become obtrusive nor so small that it is prone to being injured in normal rough-and-tumble play. The breed is just as content to sit by your side when you read or listen to music as it is to join your children for a romp in the park. Introduced early enough, the Bichon can co-exist with your cat, rabbit, or even horse as well as it can with humans. The Bichon is a breed of which it can be said without hesitation that two dogs are just as easy to raise as one.

MALE OR FEMALE?

While the sex of a dog is an important consideration in many breeds, this is not particularly the case with the Bichon. The male makes just as loving, devoted, and trainable a companion as the female.

There is one important point to consider in determining your choice between male and female—while both must be trained not to relieve themselves in the home, a male has a natural instinct to lift his leg and urinate to "mark" his home territory. It seems confusing to many dog owners, but a male's marking his home turf

A basket full of Bichon puppies has that "greeting card" appeal, but raising a puppy is a real responsibility that takes commitment on the part of the owner.

has absolutely nothing to do with whether he is housebroken. The two responses come from entirely different needs and must be dealt with in that manner. Some dogs are more difficult to train not to mark within the confines of the household than others. Males that are used for breeding are even more prone to this response and are even harder to break of it.

On the other hand, females have their semiannual "heat" cycles once they have reached sexual maturity. In the

The Bichon's amusing antics and outgoing personality can be traced back to his days as a street and circus performer.

case of the female Bichon, this occurs for the first time at about nine or ten months of age. These cycles are accompanied by vaginal discharge that creates the need to confine the female so that she does not soil her surroundings. The need for confinement of the female in heat is especially important to prevent her from becoming pregnant by some neighborhood Lothario. It must be understood that the female has no control over this bloody discharge, so it has nothing to do with training.

Both of these sexually related problems can be entirely eliminated by spaying the female and neutering the male. Unless a Bichon is purchased expressly for breeding or showing from a breeder capable of making this judgment, the dog should be sexually altered.

Breeding and raising puppies should be left in the hands of people who have the facilities to keep each and every puppy they breed until the correct homes are found for them. This can often take many months after a litter is born. Most single dog owners are not equipped to do this. Naturally, a responsible dog owner would never allow his or her pet to roam the streets and end its life in an animal shelter. Unfortunately, being forced to place a puppy due to space constraints before you are able to thoroughly check out the prospective buyer may in fact create this exact situation.

Many times we have had parents ask to buy a female "just as a pet" but with full intentions of breeding so that their children can witness "the birth process." There are countless books and videos now available that portray this wonderful event and do not add to the world-wide pet overpopulation we now face. Altering one's companion dogs not only precludes the possibility of adding to this problem, it eliminates bothersome household problems and precautions as well.

It should be understood, however, that spaying and neutering are not reversible procedures. Spayed females and neutered males are not allowed to be shown in American Kennel Club shows, nor will altered animals ever be able to be used for breeding.

THE BICHON PERSONALITY

Historically, the Bichon has been a close companion to man. Whether darling of the royal courts or circus performer, everything the Bichon has done has been done in the company of humans. The Bichon is happiest when allowed to continue that association. This is not a breed to be shut away in a kennel or outdoor run with only

"Rub my belly!" Bichons are certainly not afraid to let their owners know when they need some attention.

occasional access to your life and environment. Should this be your intent, you would be better served by another breed. The very essence of the Bichon is in his personality and sensitive nature, which is best developed by constant human contact.

Although the Bichon is certainly not a vindictive breed, we are never surprised to hear that a Bichon that has been completely housebroken will suddenly forget all of his manners in protest of suddenly being left alone too often or too long. Some Bichons will let you know that they are not getting the

The attention and affection that you give your Bichon will be worth it—he'll return your love a thousand times over.

attention they need by destroying household items, particularly those things belonging to the individual that the dog is especially devoted to if that person is "missing" too often.

None of this should be construed to mean that only those individuals who are home all day to cater to the whims of their dogs can be Bichon owners. We know many working people who are away most of the day and whose Bichons are well mannered and trustworthy when left home alone. The key here seems to be the quality, rather than quantity, of the time spent with their pets. Morning or evening walks, grooming sessions, game time, and simply having your Bichon share your life when you are home is vital to the breed's personal development and attitude. Bichons like to be talked to and praised. The old adage "No man is an island" applies to dogs as well, particularly in the case of the Bichon.

Because of his compact size and easygoing temperament, the Bichon makes a wonderful pet in any type of living quarters.

Everything about the Bichon's personality indicates that it is a non-aggressive breed. Generally speaking, the breed is somewhat submissive. We have never seen a Bichon even indicate that he would challenge his owner on any point, regardless of how much he might object to what he is being asked to do. Therefore, a stern and disapproving voice is usually more than sufficient to let your Bichon know that you disapprove of what he is doing. It is never necessary to strike your Bichon in any circumstance. A sharp "no!" is normally more than it takes to make your point.

Because of his easygoing nature, the Bichon is quite content to remain at home with his family and is not a breed that is prone to wander. However, since he is a lover of all humans, a Bichon is not beyond accepting a ride in an automobile or an invitation to play, even if the invitation comes from a total stranger.

Within the confines of his own household, however, the Bichon is an excellent watchdog in the sense that he will sound the alarm if he sees or hears anything unusual. Expect your Bichon to let you know that the doorbell has rung or that someone is knocking at the door. On the other hand, you will not be disturbed by constant and needless barking.

The Bichon makes a great effort to please his owner and is highly trainable as long as the trainer is not heavy handed. Training problems encountered are far more apt to be due to the owner rather than to the Bichon's lack of understanding or inability to learn. Although many Bichon owners are inclined to think of their companions as "little people," it must be understood that the Bichon is first and foremost *a dog*. Dogs, like the wolves from which they descended, are pack animals and they need a "pack leader." Dogs are now dependent upon humans to provide that leadership. When that leadership is not provided, an animal can easily become confused and neurotic.

Setting boundaries is important to your Bichon's well being and your relationship to him. The sooner your dog understands that there are rules that must be obeyed, the easier it will be for him to become an enjoyable companion. How soon you learn to establish and enforce those rules will determine how quickly this will come about. Don't confuse your Bichon by only enforcing your commands some of the time. It is important to a dog's well being that rules apply all of the time. Remember, the Bichon is not vindictive or particularly stubborn, but he does need guidance in order to achieve his potential.

STANDARD for the Bichon Frise

A breed standard is the criterion by which the appearance (and, to a certain extent, the temperament as well) of any given dog is made subject to objective measurement. Basically, the standard for any breed is a definition of the perfect dog to which all specimens of the breed are compared. Breed standards are always subject to change through review by the national breed club for each dog, so that it is always wise to keep up with developments in a breed by checking the publications of your national kennel club.

THE OFFICIAL STANDARD OF THE BICHON FRISE
This is the AKC standard as approved by the Bichon Frise Club of America in 1988.

General Appearance—The Bichon Frise is a small, sturdy, white powder puff of a dog whose merry temperament is evidenced by his plumed tail carried jauntily over the back and his dark-eyed inquisitive expression.

The Bichon's merry temperament should be evident in his dark-eyed, inquisitive expression. This cheerful trio is owned by Bill Dreker.

Ch. Chaminade Chamour Petrauska shows what a Bichon should look like. Owned by Barbara Stubbs and Lois Morrow.

This is a breed that has no gross or incapacitating exaggerations and therefore there is no inherent reason for lack of balance or unsound movement.

Any deviation from the ideal described in the standard should be penalized to the extent of the deviation. Structural faults common to all breeds are as undesirable in the Bichon Frise as in any other breed, even though such faults may not be specifically mentioned in the standard.

Size, Proportion, Substance—*Size*—Dogs and bitches 9 ¹/₂ to 11 ¹/₂ inches are to be given primary preference. Only where the comparative superiority of a specimen outside this range clearly justifies it should greater latitude be taken. In no case, however, should this latitude ever extend over 12 inches or under 9 inches. The minimum limits do not apply to puppies. *Proportion*—The body from the forward-most point of the chest to the point of rump is ¹/₄ longer than the height at the withers. The body from the withers to the lowest point of the chest

The Bichon's dark facial features are a contrast to his white coat and contribute to his overall pleasing expression.

represents $^1/_2$ the distance from withers to ground. *Substance*—Compact and of medium bone throughout; neither coarse nor fine.

Head—*Expression*— Soft, dark-eyed, inquisitive, alert. *Eyes* are round, black or dark brown and are set in the skull to look directly forward. An overly large or bulging eye is a fault as is an almond shaped, obliquely set eye. Halos, the black or very dark brown skin surrounding the eyes, are necessary as they accentuate the eye and enhance expression. The eye rims themselves must be black. Broken pigment, or total absence of pigment on the eye rims produce a blank and staring expression, which is a definite fault. Eyes of any color other than black or dark brown are a very serious fault and must be severely penalized. *Ears* are drop and are covered with long flowing hair. When extended toward the nose, the leathers reach approximately halfway the length of the muzzle. They are set on slightly higher than eye level and rather forward on the skull, so that when the dog is alert they serve to frame the face. The *skull* is slightly rounded, allowing for a round and forward looking eye. The *stop* is slightly accentuated. *Muzzle*—A properly balanced head is three parts muzzle to five parts skull, measured from the nose to the stop and from the stop to the occiput. A line drawn between the outside corners of the eyes and to the nose will create a near equilateral triangle. There is a slight degree of chiseling under the eyes, but not so much as to result in a weak or snipey foreface. The lower jaw is strong. The *nose* is prominent and always black. *Lips* are black, fine, never drooping. *Bite* is scissors. A bite which is undershot or overshot should be severely penalized. A crooked or out of line tooth is permissible, however, missing teeth are to be severely faulted.

Neck, Topline and Body—The arched *neck* is long and carried proudly behind an erect head. It blends smoothly into the shoulders. The length of neck from occiput to withers is approximately $^1/_3$ the

Handler Pauline Waterman proudly poses Ch. Chaminade Le Blanc Chamour. Notice the arched neck, level topline and well-developed chest that define the breed.

distance from forechest to buttocks. The *topline* is level except for a slight, muscular arch over the loin. *Body*—The chest is well developed and wide enough to allow free and unrestricted movement of the front legs. The lowest point of the chest extends at least to the elbow. The rib cage is moderately sprung and extends back to a short and muscular loin. The forechest is well pronounced and protrudes slightly forward of the point of shoulder. The underline has a moderate tuck-up. *Tail* is well plumed, set on level with the topline and curved gracefully over the back so that the hair of the tail rests on the back. When the tail is extended toward the head it reaches at least halfway to the withers. A low tail set, a tail carried perpendicularly to the back, or a tail which droops behind is to be severely penalized. A corkscrew tail is a very serious fault.

Forequarters—*Shoulders*—The shoulder blade, upper arm and forearm are approximately equal in length. The shoulders are laid back to somewhat near a forty-five degree angle. The upper arm extends well back so the elbow is placed directly below the withers when viewed

Ch. Chamour Finale was the 65th and last offspring of the great Ch. Chaminade Mr. Beau Monde to become a champion.

34

Correct coat texture is necessary —Ch. Beau Monde Miss Chaminade has the signature Bichon powder puff appearance.

from the side. *Legs* are of medium bone; straight, with no bow or curve in the forearm or wrist. The elbows are held close to the body. The *pasterns* slope slightly from the vertical. The dewclaws may be removed. The *feet* are tight and round, resembling those of a cat and point directly forward, turning neither in nor out. *Pads* are black. *Nails* are kept short.

Hindquarters—The hindquarters are of medium bone, well angulated with muscular thighs and spaced moderately wide. The upper and lower thigh are nearly equal in length meeting at a well bent stifle joint. The leg from hock joint to foot pad is perpendicular to the ground. Dewclaws may be removed. Paws are tight and round with black pads.

What a Bichon looks like during puppyhood closely reflects how he will look as an adult.

Coat—The texture of the coat is of utmost importance. The undercoat is soft and dense, the outercoat of a coarser and curlier texture. The combination of the two gives a soft but substantial feel to the touch which is similar to plush or velvet and when patted springs back. When bathed and brushed, it stands off the body, creating an overall powder puff appearance. A wiry coat is not desirable. A limp, silky coat, a coat that lies down, or a lack of undercoat are very serious faults. *Trimming*—The coat is trimmed to reveal the natural outline of the body. It is rounded off from any direction and never cut so short as to create an overly trimmed or squared off appearance. The furnishings of the head, beard, moustache, ears and tail are left longer. The longer head hair is trimmed to create an overall rounded impression. The topline is trimmed to appear level. The coat is long enough to maintain the powder puff look which is characteristic of the breed.

Color—Color is white, may have shadings of buff, cream or apricot around the ears or on the body. Any color in excess of 10% of the entire coat of a mature specimen is a fault and should be penalized, but color of the accepted shadings should not be faulted in puppies.

Gait—Movement at a trot is free, precise and effortless. In profile the forelegs and hind legs extend equally with an easy reach and drive that maintain a steady topline. When moving, the head and neck remain somewhat erect and as speed increases there is a very slight convergence of legs toward the center line. Moving away, the hindquarters travel with moderate width between them and the foot pads can be seen. Coming and going, his movement is precise and true.

Temperament—Gentle mannered, sensitive, playful and affectionate. A cheerful attitude is the hallmark of the breed and one should settle for nothing less.

An Overview of the Bichon Frise Standard

The AKC standard of the Bichon Frise is written in simple, straightforward language that can be read and understood by even the beginning fancier. What it implies, however, takes many years to fully understand. This can only be accomplished by observing many quality Bichons over the years and reading as much about the

This young Chaminade Bichon already has the look of a winner.

The Bichon's overall good looks and merry temperament make him a popular breed in the show ring and a wonderful companion dog.

breed as possible. Many books have been written about the breed and it is well worth the Bichon owner's time and effort to digest their contents if he or she is interested in showing or breeding the Bichon.

There are some breeds which change drastically from puppyhood to adulthood. It would be extremely difficult for the untrained eye to determine the actual breed of some purebred dogs in puppyhood. This is not so with the Bichon Frise. In fact, at eight weeks of age, a Bichon puppy will reflect in miniature what it will look like in many respects at maturity.

It must be remembered that a breed standard describes the "ideal" Bichon Frise, but no dog is perfect and no dog, not even the greatest dog show winner, will possess every quality asked for in its perfect form. It is how closely an individual dog adheres to the standard of the breed that determines his show potential.

One of the things that makes the Bichon Frise such an attractive dog is that even though he is not particularly large, he is a substantial dog—easily managed but not fragile in any respect. The Bichon is beautifully balanced in that it is not a low-to-the-ground breed nor is it extremely leggy or fine looking.

The Bichon's white powder-puff coat is groomed and trimmed so that it appears rounded off from any direction. The Bichon has what is referred to as a "double" coat. This means that it has a thick, woolly, and short undercoat while the outercoat is of a coarser, longer nature.

The breed standard gives a fairly wide acceptable size range: 9 1/2 to 11 1/2 inches. The average adult Bichon measures about 10 to 11 inches at the shoulder. It is important to remember that a representative Bichon never looks long in body or low to the ground. The Bichon's back is slightly shorter (measured from the highest point of the shoulders to the set on of the tail) than the measurement from shoulders to ground. The body (which is the distance from pronounced forechest to buttocks) is slightly longer than height at the shoulders.

The Bichon has an elegantly long neck, which helps to give him a classy, almost "show pony," kind of a look. This is especially apparent when a Bichon becomes curious about something and stands up on his toes and arches his long neck.

The Bichon's balanced construction permits graceful, easy movement. Since the breed standard describes very normal construction and does not call for any unusual features of construction, there should be no physical abnormalities.

Much of the breed's appeal can be found in the dark-eyed and alert expression. The Bichon's expression appears to be both interested and mischievous. The eyes are large and should be dark brown or black in color. Ideally, the eyes are surrounded by black or very dark brown pigment. The dark colored areas around the eyes are called "halos."

The pigment of the nose and lips is very dark also. The dark pigment of the eyes, nose, and lips contrasts vividly with the white coat that frames the face and gives the Bichon his distinctive look.

A happy and outgoing temperament is a hallmark of the breed and a shy or aggressive attitude is seldom found nor should it be tolerated. The well-bred and well-cared-for Bichon is always merry and bright. He is usually seen with his plumed tail wagging over his back and he seems to be inviting anyone and everyone to join him in a romp or frolic in the park.

SELECTING the Bichon for You

The Bichon you buy will live with you for many years to come. It is not the least bit unusual for the well-bred Bichon to live as long as 12, 15, or even 17 years of age. Obviously it is important that the Bichon you select has the advantage of beginning life in a healthy environment and comes from sound, healthy stock. The only way you can be sure of this is to go directly to a breeder who has earned a reputation over the years for consistently producing Bichons that are mentally and physically sound. The only way that a breeder is able to earn this reputation is through a well-planned breeding

Responsible breeders ensure that good health and temperament are passed down to each generation.

A litter of puppies is a big responsibility. It means giving each and every pup the best care right from day one.

program that has been governed by rigid selectivity. Selective breeding programs are aimed at maintaining the Bichon's many fine qualities and eliminating any genetic weaknesses.

This process is both time-consuming and costly for a breeder, but it ensures you of getting a dog that will be a joy to own. Responsible Bichon breeders protect their investments by basing their breeding programs on the healthiest, most representative stock available and providing each succeeding generation with the very best care and nutrition.

The governing kennel clubs in the different countries of the world maintain lists of local breed clubs and breeders, which can lead a prospective Bichon buyer to responsible breeders of quality stock. If you are not sure of how to contact an established Bichon breeder in your area, we strongly recommend that you call a local kennel club, your veterinarian or a local trainer for referrals.

It is highly likely that you will be able to find an established Bichon breeder in your own area. If so, you will be able to visit the breeder, inspect the premises, and, in many cases, see the puppy's parents and other relatives. These breeders are always willing and able to discuss any problems that might exist in the breed and how they should be dealt with.

Should there be no breeders in your immediate area, you can arrange to have a puppy shipped to you. There are many breeders throughout the country who have shipped puppies to satisfied owners out of state and even in other countries.

Never hesitate to ask the breeder you visit or deal with any questions or concerns you might have relative to Bichon ownership. You should expect the breeder to ask you a good number of questions as well. Good breeders are just as interested in placing their puppies in a loving and safe environment as you are in obtaining a happy, healthy puppy.

A breeder will undoubtedly want to know if there are young children in the family and if you or your children have ever owned a dog before. The breeder will want to know if you have a fenced yard and if there will be someone home during the day to attend to a young puppy's needs.

Not all good breeders maintain large kennels. In fact, you are more apt to find that Bichons come from the homes of small hobby breeders who only keep a few dogs and have litters only occasionally. The names of these people are just as likely to appear on the

An armful of baby Bichons will certainly keep your hands full! A good breeder will get to know each pup's personality to ensure that the new owners are a good match.

recommended lists from kennel clubs as the larger kennels that maintain many dogs. Hobby breeders are equally dedicated to breeding quality Bichons and have the distinct advantage of being able to raise their puppies in the home environment with the all of the accompanying personal attention and socialization.

Three of the authors' four-week-old puppies, still in the nesting box. At this age, pups' individual personalities are emerging.

Again, it is important that both the buyer and the seller ask questions. We would be highly suspicious of a person who is willing to sell you a Bichon puppy with no questions asked.

RECOGNIZING A HEALTHY PUPPY

At Drewlaine, we seldom release our puppies before they are 12 to 14 weeks of age and have been given all of their puppy inoculations. By the time the litter is eight weeks of age, it is entirely weaned (no longer nursing from the mother). While the puppies were nursing, they received antibodies from their mother that gave them complete immunity. Once they stop nursing, however, they become highly susceptible to many infectious diseases. A number of these diseases can be transmitted from the hands and clothing of humans. Therefore, it is extremely important that your puppy is current on all the shots he must have for his age.

SELECTING A PUPPY

A healthy Bichon puppy is a bouncy, playful extrovert. Never select a puppy that appears shy or listless because you feel sorry for him. Doing this will undoubtedly lead to heartache and expensive veterinary costs. Do not attempt to make up for what the breeder did not do in providing proper care and nutrition—it seldom works.

If at all possible, take the Bichon puppy you are attracted to into a different room in the kennel or house. The smells will remain the same for the puppy, so he should still feel secure, but it will give you an opportunity to see how the puppy acts away from his littermates and to inspect the puppy more closely.

Even though Bichon puppies are quite small, they should feel sturdy to the touch. They should not feel bony nor should their abdomens be bloated and extended. A puppy that has just eaten may have a full belly but the puppy should never appear obese.

A healthy puppy's ears will be pink and clean. Dark discharge or a bad odor could indicate ear mites, a sure sign of lack of cleanliness and poor maintenance. A Bichon puppy's breath should always smell sweet. His teeth must be clean and bright and there should never be any malformation of the jaw, lips, or nostrils.

Bichon eyes are dark and clear—little spots of charcoal on a snow white background. Runny eyes or eyes that appear red and irritated could be caused by a myriad of problems, none of which indicate a healthy puppy.

Coughing or diarrhea are danger signals as is any discharge from the nose or any eruptions on the skin. The fluffy little coat should be soft, clean, and lustrous.

Sound conformation can be determined as early as eight or ten weeks of age. The puppy's legs should be straight without bumps or malformations. The toes should point straight ahead.

The puppy's attitude tells you a great deal about his state of health. Puppies that are feeling "out of sorts" react very quickly and will usually find a warm littermate to snuggle up to and prefer to stay that way even when the rest of the "gang" wants to play or go exploring. The Bichon is an extrovert. Do not settle for anything less in selecting your puppy.

SELECTING A SHOW-PROSPECT PUPPY

If you or your family are considering a show career for your puppy, we strongly advise putting yourself in the hands of an established breeder who has earned a reputation for breeding winning show dogs. These breeders are the most capable of anticipating what one might expect young puppies from their lines to develop into when they reach maturity.

Although the potential buyer should read the American Kennel Club standard of perfection for the Bichon Frise, it is hard for the novice to really understand the nuances of what is being asked for. The experienced breeder is best equipped to do so and will be only too happy to assist you in your quest. However, even at that, no one can make accurate predictions or guarantees on a very young puppy.

Any predictions a breeder is apt to make are based upon the breeder's experience with past litters that produced winning show dogs. It should be obvious that the more successful a breeder has been in producing winning Bichons through the years, the broader his basis of comparison will be.

The most any responsible breeder will say about an eight-week-old puppy is that the puppy has "show potential." If you are serious about showing your Bichon, we, like most other breeders, strongly suggest waiting until a puppy is at least four or five months old before making any decisions.

There are many "beauty point" shortcomings that a Bichon puppy might have that would in no way interfere with him being a wonderful companion, but would be serious drawbacks in the show ring. Many of these things are such that a beginner in the

An experienced breeder can help predict a pup's show potential. Breeder Frank Vallely poses three-and-a-half-month-old Azara Ranza.

breed would hardly notice, which is why employing the assistance of a good breeder is so important. Still, the prospective buyer should be at least generally aware of what the Bichon show puppy should look like.

All of the foregoing regarding soundness and health apply to the show puppy as well. The show prospect must be sound and healthy, and must adhere to the standard of the breed very closely. The more you know about the history and origin of the breed, the better equipped you will be to see the differences that distinguish the show dog from the pet.

Like the pet, the show prospect puppy must have a happy, outgoing temperament. He will be a compact little bundle of fluff, never appearing short-legged or out of balance. The show puppy will move around with ease, his head held high and his tail carried over the back. Dark eyes, a dark nose, and dark lips are important.

Though a pure white coat is preferred, many puppies have shadings of cream or apricot in their coats. In most cases, this color disappears entirely by the time the puppy has reached adulthood. The breeder from whom you purchase your Bichon will be able to tell you what to expect in regard to this "puppy color."

PUPPY OR ADULT?

For the person anticipating a show career for their Bichon or for someone hoping to become a breeder, the purchase of a young adult provides greater certainty with respect to quality. Even those who simply want a companion could consider the adult dog. In some instances, breeders will have males or females they no longer wish to use for breeding and after the dogs have been altered, the breeders would prefer to have the dogs live out their lives in private homes with all of the attendant care and attention.

Acquiring an adult dog eliminates the

In selecting a Bichon Frise, you must consider whether a puppy or an adult would better fit your lifestyle.

Keep a close eye on what your Bichon puppy gets into. A stick may be a tempting treat for a teething pup, but it can break into small, potentially dangerous pieces.

many problems that raising a puppy involves and Bichons are a breed that "transfer" well. They love to be with humans and, though many of us hate to admit it, most Bichons are just as content living with one person as they would be with another as long as they are well cared for.

Elderly people often prefer adult dogs, particularly ones that are housebroken in that they are easier to manage and require less supervision and damage control. Adult Bichons are seldom "chewers" and are usually more than ready to adapt to household rules.

There are things to consider, though. Adult dogs have usually developed behaviors that may or may not fit into your routine. If a Bichon has never been exposed to small children, the dog may be totally perplexed, and often frightened, by this new experience. Children are inclined to be more active and vocal than the average adult and this could intimidate the dog as well.

We strongly advise taking an adult dog on a trial basis to see if the dog will adapt to your lifestyle and environment. Most often it works, but on rare occasions a prospective owner decides that training his dog from puppyhood is worth the time and effort it requires.

IDENTIFICATION PAPERS

The purchase of any purebred dog entitles you to three very important documents: a health record that includes an inoculation

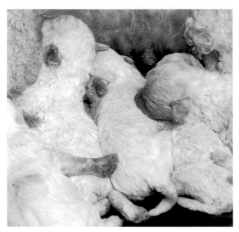

The antibodies in their mother's milk protect the pups from disease until they are old enough to be vaccinated.

record, a copy of the dog's pedigree, and the dog's registration certificate.

You will find that most Bichon breeders have initiated the necessary preliminary inoculation series for their puppies by the time they are eight weeks of age. These inoculations temporarily protect the puppies against hepatitis, leptospirosis, distemper, and canine parvovirus. "Permanent" inoculations will follow at a prescribed time. Since different breeders and veterinarians follow different approaches to inoculations, it is important that the health record you obtain for your puppy accurately lists what shots have been given and when. In this way, the veterinarian you choose will be able to continue on with the appropriate inoculation series as needed. In most cases, rabies inoculations are not given until a puppy is six months of age or older.

The pedigree is your dog's "family tree." The breeder must supply you with a copy of this document, which authenticates your puppy's ancestors back to at least the third generation.

The registration certificate is the canine world's "birth certificate." This certificate is issued by a country's governing kennel club. When you transfer the ownership of your Bichon from the breeder's name to your own name, the transaction is entered on this certificate. Once the certificate is mailed to the appropriate kennel club, the information is permanently recorded in their computerized files.

Keep all of your dog's documents in a safe place, as you will need them when you visit your veterinarian or if you should ever wish to breed or show your Bichon. Keep the name, address, and phone number of the breeder from whom you purchased your Bichon in a separate place as well. Should you ever lose any of these important documents, you will then be able to contact the breeder regarding obtaining duplicates.

DIET SHEET

Your Bichon is the happy healthy puppy he is because the breeder has been carefully feeding him and caring for him. Every breeder we know has his own particular way of doing this. Most breeders give the new owners written records that detail the amounts and kinds of food that the puppies have been receiving. Follow these recommendations to the letter at least for the first month or two after the puppy comes to live with you.

The diet sheet should indicate the number of times a day your Bichon is accustomed to being fed and the kind of vitamin supplementation, if any, he has been receiving. Following the prescribed procedure will reduce the chance of upset stomach and loose stools.

Usually a breeder's diet sheet projects the increases and changes in food that will be necessary as your puppy grows from week to week. If the sheet does not include this information, ask the breeder for suggestions regarding increases and the eventual changeover to adult food.

In the unlikely event that you are not supplied with a diet sheet by the breeder and are unable to get one, your veterinarian will be able to advise you in this respect. There are countless foods that are now being manufactured expressly to meet the nutritional needs of

A breeder's diet sheet helps new owners to continue feeding the pups a nutritionally sound diet as they grow.

puppies and growing dogs. A trip down the pet aisle at your supermarket or to your local pet store will prove just how many choices you have. Two important tips to remember: read labels carefully for content and, when dealing with established, reliable manufacturers, you are more likely to get what you pay for.

HEALTH GUARANTEE

Any reputable breeder is more than willing to supply a written agreement that the purchase of your Bichon is contingent upon the dog's passing a veterinarian's examination. Ideally, you will be able to arrange an appointment with your chosen veterinarian right after you have picked up your puppy from the breeder and before you take the puppy home. If this is not possible, you should not delay seeing the veterinarian longer than 24 hours from the time you take your puppy home.

TEMPERAMENT AND SOCIALIZATION

Temperament is both hereditary and learned. Inherited good temperament can be ruined by poor treatment and lack of proper socialization. A Bichon puppy that comes from shy or nervous stock or that exhibits those characteristics himself will make a poor companion or show dog, and should certainly never be bred. Therefore, it is critical that you obtain a happy puppy from a breeder who is determined to produce good temperaments and who has taken all the necessary steps to provide the necessary early socialization.

Temperaments in the same litter can range from confident and outgoing on the high end of the scale to shy and fearful at the low end. However, the large majority of Bichon temperaments are and should be delightful. Cheerful temperament is a hallmark of the breed.

Early socialization takes place within the litter as the pups interact with their dam and with each other.

A very important aspect of socialization is human contact. Puppies need exposure to and attention from all types of people in order to become well adjusted.

If you are fortunate enough to have children in the household or living nearby, your socialization task will be assisted considerably. Bichons raised with children are the best. The two seem to understand each other and, in some way known only to the puppies and the children themselves, they give each other the confidence to face the trying ordeal of growing up.

The children in your own household are not the only children your Bichon should spend time with. It is a case of the more the merrier! Every child (and adult for that matter) that enters your household should be introduced to your Bichon. If trustworthy children live nearby, have them take the puppy on short walks. If there is adult supervision, an afternoon visit to a neighbor with children is a grand idea as well!

Your puppy should go everywhere with you: the post office, the market, the shopping mall, wherever. Be prepared to create a stir wherever you go, because the attraction that you had for the first Bichon you met applies to other people as well. Everyone will want to pet your little "cotton ball" and there is nothing in the world better for your puppy.

Should your puppy back off from a stranger, pick him up and hand him to the person. The young Bichon will quickly learn that all humans—young and old, short and tall, and of all races—are friends.

If your Bichon has a show career in his future, there are other things in addition to just being handled that will have to be taught. All Bichon show dogs must learn to have their mouths inspected by the judge. The judge must also be able to check their teeth. Males must be accustomed to having their testicles touched as dog show judges must determine that all male dogs are "complete," which means that there are two normal-sized testicles in the scrotum. These inspections must begin in puppyhood and be done on a regular and continuing basis.

Bichons seem to be entirely compatible with other dogs as well as with humans. If you are fortunate enough to have a dog park nearby, visit it with your puppy as frequently as possible, daily if time permits. A young Bichon that has been exposed regularly to other dogs from puppyhood will learn to adapt and accept other dogs and other breeds much more readily than a Bichon that seldom ever sees strange dogs.

THE ADOLESCENT BICHON

Bichons attain their full height fairly quickly. Usually by 10 or 11 months of age a Bichon has grown as tall as it will get. However,

at that age, the dog is far from mature. Some Bichon lines achieve maturity at around two years of age. Others are almost three before they are fully developed.

At about nine or ten months of age, the adult coat begins to emerge. You will notice a change in hair texture on the

An affectionate Bichon pup is a little bundle of unconditional love!

Bichon's back, near the tail. Prior to that time,

Bichons are known for being friendly and compatible with most other dogs — as demonstrated by this young Bichon who plants a kiss on his friend's muzzle!

the Bichon's puppy coat is soft, silky, and relatively thin. The new hair that comes in will be of a much coarser texture. Up until this time, the puppy coat is relatively easy to care for. Thorough brushing will only take a few minutes two or three times a week.

It is important, however, that you attend to these grooming sessions regularly during the early months of your Bichon's growth. The coat change period will require more of your time because the dead puppy hair is loosening and being replaced by new adult hair. Mats occur easily and frequently during this time. If your Bichon has been groomed regularly, you will find that your task is much easier.

Food needs change during this adolescent growth period. Some Bichons seem as if they can never get enough to eat while others eat just enough to avoid starving. Think of Bichon puppies as being as individualistic as children and act accordingly.

The amount of food you give your Bichon should be adjusted to how much he will readily consume at each meal. If the entire meal is eaten quickly, add a small amount to the next feeding and continue to do so as the need increases. This method will ensure you of giving your puppy enough food, but you must also pay close

The care and socialization that you give your Bichon when he is young will shape his personality and behavior for the rest of his life.

attention to the puppy's appearance and condition as you do not want him to become overweight or obese.

At eight weeks of age, a Bichon puppy is eating four meals a day. By the time he is six months old, the puppy can do well on two meals a day with perhaps a snack in the middle of the day. If your puppy does not eat the food he is offered, he is either not hungry or not well. Your dog will eat when he is hungry. If you suspect that the dog is not well, a trip to the veterinarian is in order.

You will have to keep up with your pup's changing grooming needs and nutritional requirements.

This adolescent period is particularly important, as it is the time that your Bichon must learn all of the household and social rules by which he will live for the rest of his life. Your patience and commitment during this time will not only produce a respected canine good citizen but will also forge a bond between the two of you that will grow and ripen into a wonderful relationship.

CARING for Your Bichon Frise

The best way to make sure that your Bichon puppy is obtaining the right amount and the correct type of food for his age is to follow the diet sheet provided by the breeder from whom you purchased your puppy. Do your best not to change the puppy's diet and he will be less apt to run into digestive problems and diarrhea. Diarrhea is very serious in young puppies. Puppies with diarrhea can dehydrate very rapidly, causing severe problems and even death.

If it is necessary to change your Bichon puppy's diet for any reason, it should be done gradually over a period of several meals and a few days. Begin by adding a tablespoon or two of the new food and taking away the same amount of the old food, gradually increasing the amount until the meal consists entirely of the new product.

By the time your Bichon is 10 to 12 months old, you can reduce feedings to once a day. This meal can be given either in the morning or evening. It is really a matter of choice on your part. There are two important things to remember: feed the main meal at the same time every day and make sure what you feed is nutritionally complete.

The single meal can be supplemented by a morning or nighttime snack of hard dog biscuits made especially for smaller dogs. These biscuits not only become highly anticipated treats but are also genuinely helpful in maintaining your Bichon's healthy gums and teeth.

Good nutrition will be evident in your dog's healthy appearance and enthusiastic attitude.

BALANCED DIETS

In order for a canine diet to qualify as "complete and balanced" in the United States, it must meet standards set by the American Association of Feed Control Officials (AAFCO). Most commercial foods manufactured for dogs meet these standards and prove this by listing the ingredients contained in the food on every package or can. The ingredients are listed in descending order with the main ingredient listed first. Fed with any regularity at

The two most important things to remember about feeding your Bichon are to make sure that what you feed is nutritionally complete and to follow a set feeding schedule.

all, refined sugars can cause your Bichon to become obese and will definitely create tooth decay. Candy stores do not exist in the wild and canine teeth are not genetically disposed to handling sugars. Do not feed your Bichon candy or sweets and avoid products that contain sugar to any high degree.

Fresh water and a properly prepared balanced diet that contains the essential nutrients in correct proportions are all that a healthy Bichon needs. Dog foods come canned, dry, semi-moist, "scientifically fortified," and "all-natural." A visit to your local supermarket or pet store will reveal how vast an array you will be able to select from.

It is important to remember that all dogs, whether they are Bichons or Great Danes, are carnivorous (meat-eating) animals. While the vegetable content of your Bichon's diet should not be overlooked, a dog's physiology and anatomy are based upon carnivorous food acquisition. Protein and fat are absolutely essential to the well-being of your Bichon.

Read the list of ingredients on the dog food you buy. Animal protein should appear first on the label's list of ingredients. A base of quality kibble to which meat and even table scraps have been added can provide a nutritious meal for your Bichon.

This having been said, it should be realized that in the wild, when a carnivore captures and kills an animal, it uses the entire animal for food. The carnivore's kills consist almost entirely of herbivores (plant-eaters) and invariably the carnivore begins its meal with the contents of the herbivore's stomach. This provides the carbohydrates, minerals, and nutrients present in vegetables.

Through centuries of domestication we have made our dogs entirely dependent upon us for their well-being. Therefore, we are entirely responsible for duplicating the food balance that the wild dog finds in nature. The domesticated dog's diet must include protein, carbohydrates, fats, roughage, and small amounts of essential minerals and vitamins.

Finding commercially prepared diets that contain all of the necessary nutrients will not present a problem. It is important to understand, though, that these commercially prepared foods do contain all the necessary nutrients that your Bichon needs. It is therefore unnecessary to add vitamin supplements to these diets unless specially prescribed by your veterinarian. Over-supplementation and forced growth are now looked upon by some breeders as major contributors to many skeletal abnormalities found in today's purebred dogs.

Jake and his "catch of the day." Things could get a little messy if your Bichon chooses his own food; it's best for you to provide him with the nutrition that he needs.

Good oral care and nutritious safe treats are important to your dog's health and well-being.

OVER-SUPPLEMENTATION

A great deal of controversy exists today regarding orthopedic problems such as hip and patella (knee) dysplasia that afflict Bichons and many other breeds. Some claim that these problems are entirely hereditary conditions but many others feel that they can be exacerbated by excessive use of mineral and vitamin supplements for puppies.

In giving vitamin supplementation, one should *never* exceed the prescribed amount. Many Bichon breeders insist that all recommended dosages be halved before including them in a dog's diet. Still other breeders feel that no supplementation should be given at all, believing that a balanced diet, including plenty of dairy products and a small amount of bone meal to provide calcium, is all that is necessary and beneficial.

Pregnant and lactating bitches may require supplementation of some kind, but here again it is not a case of "if a little is good, a lot would be a great deal better." Extreme caution is advised in this case and the situation is best discussed with your veterinarian.

The hot sun and high temperatures can be dangerous for the Bichon, but that's no problem for this pup, who prefers lounging in the shade.

If the owner of a Bichon normally eats healthy nutritious food, there is no reason why the dog cannot be given table scraps. What could possibly be harmful in good nutritious food? Table scraps should be given only as part of the dog's meal and never from the table. A Bichon that becomes accustomed to being hand-fed from the table can become a real pest at meal time. Also, dinner guests may find the pleading stare of your Bichon less than appealing when dinner is being served.

Dogs do not care if food looks like a hot dog or a piece of cheese. Truly nutritious dog foods are seldom manufactured to look like food that appeals to humans. Dogs only care about how food smells and tastes. It is highly doubtful that you will be eating your dog's food, so do not waste your money on these "looks just like" products.

Along these lines, most of the moist or canned foods that have the look of "delicious red beef" look that way because they contain large amounts of red dyes. They should not be fed to a Bichon Frise!

The same coloring that makes these products look red will stain and discolor your Bichon's beard. Some breeders claim that these products can cause tearing, which could stain your Bichon's entire face.

To test the dye content of either canned or dry foods, place a small amount of the food after it has been prepared for your dog on an absorbent towel and allow it to remain there for several hours. If the paper is stained, you can rest assured that your dog's coat will be stained as well. Further, preservatives and dyes are no better for your dog than they are for you.

SPECIAL DIETS

There are now a number of commercially prepared diets for dogs with special dietary needs. Overweight, underweight, or geriatric dogs can have their nutritional needs met, as can puppies and growing dogs. The calorie content of these foods is adjusted accordingly. With the correct amount of the right foods and the proper amount of exercise, your Bichon should stay in top shape. Again, common sense must prevail. Too many calories will increase

A nutritionally balanced puppy food and lots of fresh water are all that a growing Bichon needs in terms of diet. Supplementation at too early an age can do more harm than good.

weight, too few will reduce weight.

Occasionally, a young Bichon going through the teething period will become a poor eater. The concerned owner's first response is to tempt the dog by hand-feeding special treats and foods that the problem eater seems to prefer. This practice only serves to compound the problem. Once the dog learns to play the waiting game, he will turn up his nose at anything other than his favorite food, knowing full well that what it *wants* to eat will eventually arrive.

Unlike humans, dogs have no suicidal tendencies. A healthy dog will not starve himself to death. He may not eat enough to keep himself in the shape we find ideal and attractive, but he will definitely eat enough to maintain himself. If your Bichon is not eating properly and appears to be too thin, it is probably best to consult your veterinarian

SPECIAL NEEDS OF THE BICHON

Exercise

If your own exercise proclivities are closer to a walk around the

While the Bichon is not a breed that requires excessive exercise, every dog needs some activity or else he may find less constructive ways to release his energy.

If you have more than one dog, they will enjoy playing with each other, especially if you initiate the game.

block than to marathon runs, your choice of a Bichon was probably a wise one. The Bichon is not a breed that requires taking your energy level to its outer limits. In fact, if your Bichon shares his life with young children or other dogs, he could easily be getting all the exercise he needs to stay fit. A Bichon is always ready for a romp or even to invent some new game that entails plenty of aerobic activity.

This does not mean that your Bichon will not benefit from a brisk daily walk or a moderate jog around the park. On the contrary, slow steady exercise that keeps your companion's heart at a working rate will do nothing but extend his life. If your Bichon is doing all of this with you at his side, you are increasing the chances that the two of you will enjoy each other's company for many more years to come.

Naturally, common sense must be used in determining the extent and the intensity of the exercise you give your Bichon. Remember, young puppies have short bursts of energy and then need long periods of rest. No puppy of any breed should be forced to accompany you on extended runs, as serious injuries can result. Again, short exercise periods and long rest stops are necessary for any Bichon under 10 or 12 months of age.

Most adult Bichons will willingly walk as far, perhaps even farther, than their owners are inclined to go. Daily walks combined with some retrieving or game-playing in the yard can keep the average Bichon in fine condition.

Hot Weather

Caution must be exercised in hot weather. First of all, the Bichon is not a breed that enjoys being exposed to hot summer sun. Plan your walks for the first thing in the morning, if at all possible. If you cannot arrange to do this, wait until the sun has set and the outdoor temperature has dropped to a comfortable degree.

You must *never* leave your Bichon in a car in hot weather. Temperatures can soar in a matter of minutes and your dog can die of heat exhaustion in less time than you would ever imagine. Rolling down the windows only helps a little and is dangerous in that an overheated Bichon will panic and attempt to escape through the open window. A word to the wise—leave your Bichon at home in a cool room on hot days.

Cold weather, even temperatures hovering around the zero mark, is no problem at all for the Bichon. The only warm clothing required for your winter walks will be yours as long as the two of you keep moving. Do not, however, remain wet if the two of you get caught in the rain. At the very least you should towel dry the wet Bichon. Better still, use your blow dryer to make sure that your Bichon is thoroughly dry and mat-free.

Gio and Pookie are two "couch potatoes" who share a favorite resting spot.

Socialization

The Bichon is a happy dog by nature and he takes most situations in stride. However, it is important to accommodate the breed's natural instincts by making sure that your dog is accus-tomed to everyday events of all kinds. Traffic, strange noises, loud or hyperactive children, and strange animals can be very

A naturally inquisitive Bichon pup has no trouble keeping himself busy and active.

intimidating to a dog of any breed that has never experienced them before. Gently and gradually introduce your Bichon puppy to as many strange situations as you possibly can.

Make it a practice to take your Bichon with you everywhere whenever it is practical. Be prepared to be stopped by passers-by when you are out with your Bichon. The breed is a real crowd pleaser and you will find that your Bichon will savor all of the attention it gets.

GROOMING Your Bichon Frise

Much of what initially attracts people to the Bichon Frise is in his jaunty tailored look. We wish we could tell you that look is a natural part of the breed's inheritance but, unfortunately, it is not. Your Bichon will only maintain that special look as long as you are diligent in keeping his coat thoroughly brushed, his beard and whiskers clean, and either trimming his coat yourself or finding a talented groomer. This cannot be accomplished by occasional attacks on the problem after long periods of neglect.

The damage done by neglecting the Bichon's coat can normally only be undone by shaving away the coat because of the mats that have developed. This is neither attractive nor is it good for your dog. If you are not willing to put in the time and effort necessary to maintain the Bichon's coat, which to a great extent constitutes his very essence, why not get a smooth-coated dog instead?

Do not think you are doing your dog a favor by shaving him. The Bichon's coat insulates against both heat and cold. Shaving your dog to keep him cool for the summer months is working against the breed's natural defense against soaring temperatures.

It is not necessary to maintain the *length* of coat that the Bichon needs for the show ring, but keeping the *shape* of the breed is important.

PUPPY COAT

Undoubtedly the breeder from whom you purchased your Bichon began to accustom the puppy to grooming just as soon as there was enough hair to brush. You must continue on with grooming sessions or begin them at once if for some reason they have not been already started. You and your Bichon will spend many hours involved with this activity over a lifetime, so it is imperative that both of you learn to cooperate in order to make grooming an easy and pleasant experience.

The first piece of equipment you will have to obtain is a grooming table. A grooming table can be built or purchased at your local pet supply store. A sturdy card table topped with a non-skid pad can be used, but the larger the area the dog stands on, the more apt he is to want to wander.

The distinctive look of the Bichon's coat doesn't come naturally. It requires diligent care on a regular basis, either by the owner or a professional groomer.

Make sure that whatever kind of table you use is of a height at which you can work comfortably. Adjustable-height grooming tables are available at most pet shops. Although you will buy the table when your Bichon puppy first arrives, anticipate his full grown size in making your purchase and select or build a table that will accommodate a fully grown Bichon lying on his side.

You will also need to invest in two brushes, a steel comb, barber's scissors, and a pair of nail clippers. Consider the fact that you will be using this equipment for many years, so buy the best of these items that you can afford.

The two brushes that you will need are a wire "slicker brush" (also called a "rake") and a pin brush, sometimes called a "Poodle brush."

Do not attempt to groom your puppy on the floor. The puppy will only attempt to get away from you when he has decided that enough is enough and you will spend a good part of your time chasing him around the room. Besides, sitting on the floor for long stretches of time is not the most comfortable position for the average adult.

The Bichon puppy should be taught to lie on his side to be groomed. As your Bichon grows and develops his adult coat, you will find that the bit of effort you invested in teaching him to lie on

Since grooming is such a large part of the Bichon's care and maintenance, it is best to accustom him to the procedure at as early an age as possible.

Combing the sensitive area around the puppy's face must be done with great care in order not to hurt the puppy and not to pull or break the hair

his side will be time well spent, as he will be kept in that position for most of the brushing process. The Bichon will have to be kept in the standing position for trimming, but the lying position is a bit more difficult for the puppy to learn.

Begin training the puppy to lie down by putting him down on his side on the table. Speak reassuringly to the puppy, stroking his head and rump. Do this a number of times before you attempt to do any grooming. Repeat the process until your puppy understands what he is supposed to do when you place him on the grooming table.

To brush the puppy coat, start with the slicker brush and begin what is called "line brushing" at the top of the shoulder. Part the hair in a straight line from the front of the shoulder straight down to the bottom of the chest. Brush through the hair to the right and left of the part. Start at the skin and brush out to the very ends of the hair. Do a small section at a time and continue down the part. When you reach the bottom of the part, return to the top and make another part just to the right of the

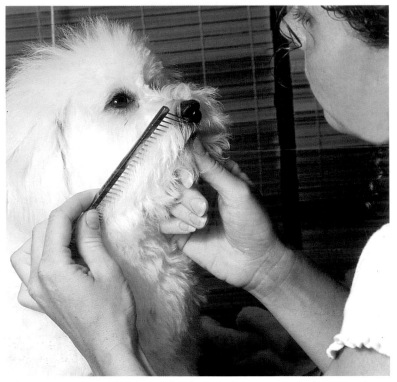

If you encounter a mat that does not brush out easily, try to separate the hairs with your fingers and a steel comb.

first line you brushed. *Part and brush.* You will repeat this process, working toward the rear, until you reach the puppy's tail.

I prefer to do the legs on the same side I have been working on at the time. Using the same process, part the hair at the top of the leg and work down. Do this all around each leg and be especially careful to attend to the hard-to-reach areas under the upper legs where they join the body. Mats occur in these areas very rapidly, especially when the Bichon is shedding his puppy coat.

Should you encounter a mat that does not brush out easily, use your fingers and the steel comb to separate the hairs as much as possible. Do not cut or pull out the matted hair. Apply baby powder or one of the specially prepared grooming powders directly to the mat and brush completely from the skin out.

When you have finished one side, including the legs, turn the puppy over and complete the entire process on the other side—*part and brush.* As your Bichon becomes accustomed to this process, you may find that the puppy considers this nap time. You may have to lift your puppy into the standing position to arouse him from his slumber.

With the puppy standing, do the chest and tail. When brushing the longer hair of the tail and face, be gentle so as not to break the hair. When brushing on and around the rear legs, be sure to give special attention to the area of the anus and genitalia. Needless to say, it is important to be extremely careful when brushing these areas as they are very sensitive and easily injured.

NAIL TRIMMING

This is a good time to accustom your Bichon to having his nails trimmed and having his feet inspected. Always inspect your dog's feet for cracked pads. Check between the toes for splinters and thorns. Pay particular attention to any swollen or tender areas. In many areas of the country, there is a weed that releases a small barbed "hook" that carries its seed. This hook can easily find its way into a Bichon's foot or between his toes, and will very quickly work its way deep into the dog's flesh. This will very quickly cause soreness and infection These barbs are should be removed by your veterinarian before serious problems result.

The time you put into grooming your Bichon puppy will be worth it when you see the finished product.

The nails of a Bichon who spends most of his time indoors, or on grass when outdoors, can grow long very quickly. If your Bichon is getting plenty of exercise on cement or rough hard pavement, the nails may keep sufficiently worn down. Otherwise, the nails will grow long and will have to be trimmed with canine nail clippers.

Do not allow the nails to become overgrown and then expect to cut them back easily. Each nail has a blood vessel running through its center called the "quick." The quick grows close to the end of the nail and contains very sensitive nerve endings. If the nail is allowed to grow too long, it will be impossible to cut it back to a proper length without cutting into the quick. Cutting the quick causes severe pain to the dog and can also result in a great deal of bleeding that can be very difficult to stop.

Should the quick be nipped in the trimming process, there are a number of blood clotting products available at pet shops that will almost immediately stem the flow of blood. It is wise to have one of these products on hand in case there is a nail trimming accident or the dog tears a nail on his own.

GROOMING THE ADULT BICHON

Fortunately, you and your Bichon have spent the many months between puppyhood and full maturity learning to assist each other through the grooming process. The two of you have survived the changing of the puppy coat and the arrival of the adult coat. Not only is the Bichon's adult hair of an entirely different texture, it is much longer and much thicker.

Brushing the Bichon's adult coat is the same as brushing the puppy coat with one obvious difference—longer, thicker hair.

By this time, you have undoubtedly realized that the pin brush, with its longer bristles set in rubber, is far more effective for line-brushing the adult Bichon than the slicker

Try to make your puppy as comfortable as possible while you clip his nails. Once he realizes that nail clipping is a painless procedure, it will become second nature.

brush that you used through puppyhood. The pin brush is also less apt to tear out the adult Bichon's longer hair.

The method of brushing the adult coat is the same method that you have been using since your Bichon was a puppy. The obvious difference is that you have more dog and more hair. While one might expect grooming an adult Bichon to be a monumental task; this is not necessarily so. The two of you have been practicing the brushing routine for so long that it has undoubtedly become second nature to both of you. Ten industriously applied minutes a day with a brush, plus a thorough weekly session, will keep your Bichon entirely mat-free.

BATHING

A Bichon should never be bathed until after he has been thoroughly brushed. A matted Bichon will only get worse when doused with water.

A spray hose is necessary to thoroughly wet the Bichon's thick coat, as well as to remove any shampoo residue.

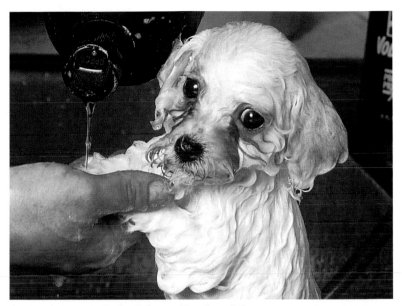

Soap and rinse your Bichon's face and head carefully, paying attention not to get soap in the dog's eyes.

A rubber mat should be placed at the bottom of the tub to keep your Bichon from slipping and thereby becoming frightened. A rubber spray hose is absolutely necessary to thoroughly wet the adult Bichon's coat. The hose is also necessary to remove all shampoo residue.

A small cotton ball placed inside each ear will keep water from running down into the dog's ear canals, and a drop or two of mineral oil or a dab of petroleum jelly placed in each eye will preclude shampoo irritating the Bichon's eyes.

It is best to use a shampoo designed especially for white dogs. To bathe your Bichon, start behind the ears and work back. Use a wash cloth to soap and rinse around the head and face. Once you have shampooed your Bichon, you must rinse the coat thoroughly and, when you feel quite certain that all shampoo residue has been removed, rinse once more. Shampoo residue in the coat is sure to dry the hair and could cause skin irritation.

As soon as you have completed the bath, use heavy towels to remove as much of the excess water as possible. Your Bichon will assist you in the process by shaking a great deal of the water out of his coat on his own.

USING A HAIR DRYER

It is very important to "brush dry" your Bichon using your pin brush and a hair dryer if you also plan on trimming the dog yourself. Allowing the Bichon's hair to dry on its own will cause the hair to curl, making it absolutely impossible to scissor the coat properly.

A dryer that has its own stand is well worth the investment with this breed. It will simplify the task by allowing you to use both of your hands to do the line brushing, and it will cut the time it takes to dry the dog in half.

Right after a quick towel drying, use your pin brush to go through the damp coat and remove any tangles. Always set your hair dryer on the "medium" setting, never on "hot." The hot setting may be quicker, but it will also dry out your Bichon's hair and could easily burn his skin.

With your Bichon lying on his side, use the line brushing method that you used before the bath. Point the dryer at the area

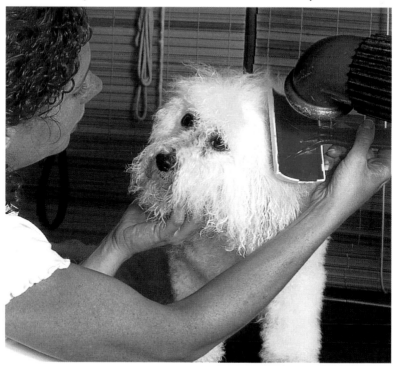

"Brush drying" your Bichon is essential if you plan on trimming his coat; letting the coat air dry causes the hair to curl and makes it impossible to scissor properly.

to be brushed and use light strokes repeatedly until that section is completely dry, then move on to the next section. Brush gently and be careful not to pull the hair out.

As soon as your Bichon is dry, begin the trimming process immediately or the hair will start to curl and all of your brush-drying efforts will be wasted.

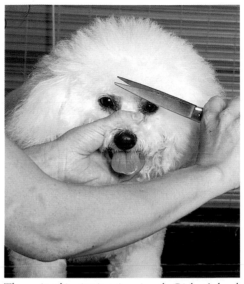

The main objective in trimming the Bichon's head hair is to create a rounded look.

Scissoring

The main difference between the pet trim and the show trim is primarily in the length of the hair, but the finish work involved in the show trim is truly an art that takes years of training and practice. The pet trim is much shorter and easier to maintain. If you plan to show your Bichon, we strongly advise you to go to a professional groomer who is an expert at trimming the breed for the show ring.

For home purposes, practice makes perfect. Remember that the hair of the beard, ears, and tail is always kept much longer than the rest of the coat. The actual length depends upon what you find easiest to maintain. When you are trimming your Bichon's head, the object is to create a rounded look without any indentation where the ears join the head. Though this sounds unimportant, it is one of the things that differentiates the Bichon's look from that of the Poodle.

Look at the pictures of the well-groomed Bichons in this book and try to create the same shape on your own dog. A tip to remember is to constantly lift the hair up with your comb as go along, as this will keep all of the hairs standing directly away from the dog's body. With practice, you will be able to achieve the smooth but plush look that you are after.

TRAINING Your Bichon Frise

There is no breed of dog that cannot be trained. It does appear that some breeds are more difficult to get the desired response from than others. In many cases, however, this has more to do with the trainer and his training methods than with the dog's inability to learn. With the proper approach, any dog that is not mentally deficient can be taught to be a good canine citizen. Many dog owners do not understand how a dog learns nor do they realize that they can be breed-specific in their approach to training.

Young puppies have an amazing capacity to learn. This capacity is greater than most humans realize. It is important to remember, though, that these young puppies also forget with great speed unless they are reminded of what they have learned by continual reinforcement.

As puppies leave the nest, they began their search for two things: a pack leader and the rules set down by that leader by which they can abide. Because puppies, particularly Bichon puppies, are cuddly and cute, their owners fail miserably in supplying these very basic canine needs. Instead, the owner immediately begins to respond to the demands of the puppy.

It's hard to be strict with a puppy as cute as the Bichon, but it's important that you call the shots and never let your puppy get the upper "paw."

Bichons are natural detectives—they will stick their noses into anything and everything if they're not taught what is off-limits.

For example, if you let a puppy in the house every time he barks or whines, he will quickly learn that he is being allowed into the house *because* he is barking or whining. Instead of learning that the only way he will be fed is to follow a set procedure (i.e., sitting or lying down on command) he learns that leaping about the kitchen is what gets results.

If the young puppy cannot find his pack leader in an owner, the puppy assumes the role of pack leader himself. If there are no rules imposed, the puppy learns to make his own rules. And, unfortunately, the negligent owner continually reinforces the puppy's decisions by allowing him to govern the household.

With small dogs like our Bichon, this scenario can produce a neurotic nuisance. In large dogs, the situation can be downright dangerous. Neither situation is an acceptable one.

The key to successful training lies in establishing the proper relationship between dog and owner. The owner or the owning family must be the pack leader, and the pack leader must provide the rules by which the dog abides.

Once this is established, ease of training depends a great deal upon just how much a dog relies on his master's approval. The entirely dependent dog lives to please his master and will do everything in his power to evoke the approval response from the person he is devoted to.

At the opposite end of the spectrum, we have the totally independent dog who is not remotely concerned with what his master thinks. Dependency varies from one breed to the next and, to a degree, within breeds as well. Bichons are no exception to this rule, but, fortunately for the Bichon owner, the breed is far more dependent than many others.

HOUSEBREAKING

The Crate Method

A major key to successfully training your Bichon, whether it is obedience training or housebreaking, is *avoidance.* It is much easier for your Bichon to learn something if you do not first have to have him unlearn some bad habit. The crate training method of housebreaking is a highly successful method of preventing bad habits from ever beginning.

First time dog owners are inclined to initially see the crate, or cage, method of housebreaking as cruel, but those same people will return later and thank us profusely for having suggested it in the first place. They are also surprised to find that the puppy will eventually come to think of his crate as a special retreat—a den in which he can rest and find privacy. The success of the crate method is based upon the fact that puppies will not soil the area in which they sleep unless they are forced to.

Use of a crate reduces house training time down to an absolute minimum and avoids keeping a puppy under constant stress by incessantly correcting him for making mistakes in the house. The anti-crate advocates consider it cruel to confine a puppy for any length of time, but they find no problem in constantly harassing and punishing the puppy because he has wet on the carpet and relieved himself behind the sofa.

Crates come in a wide variety of styles. The fiberglass shipping kennels used by many airlines are popular with Bichon owners, but residents of the warmer climates sometimes prefer the wire-type crates. Both types are available at pet stores.

There are also many sizes to choose from. The medium size (approximately 20 inches high by 24 inches wide by 30 inches long) seems ideal for most Bichons.

The crate used for housebreaking should only be large enough for the puppy to stand up, lie down, and stretch out comfortably in. It is not necessary to dash out and buy a new crate every few weeks to accommodate the Bichon's rapid spurts of growth. Simply cut a piece of plywood to partition off the excess space in the crate and move it back as needed. Long before you have lost the need for the partition, your Bichon will be housebroken—I assure you.

Begin feeding your Bichon puppy in the crate. Keep the door closed and latched while the puppy is eating. When the meal is finished, open the crate and *carry* the puppy outdoors to the spot where you want it to learn to eliminate. In the event that you do not have outdoor access or will be away from home for long periods of time, begin housebreaking by placing newspapers in

Make sure your Bichon has plenty of time to eliminate outside during the housetraining process.

some out of the way corner that is easily accessible for the puppy. If you consistently take your puppy to the same spot, you will reinforce the habit of going there for that purpose.

It is important that you do not let the puppy loose after eating. Young puppies will eliminate almost immediately after eating or drinking. They will also be ready to relieve themselves when they first wake up and after playing. If you keep a watchful eye on your puppy, you will quickly learn when this is about to take place. A puppy usually circles and sniffs the floor just before it will relieve himself. Do not give your puppy an opportunity to learn that he can eliminate in the house! Your house training chores will be reduced considerably if you avoid this happening in the first place.

If you are not able to watch your puppy every minute, he should be in his crate with the door securely latched. Each time you put your puppy in the crate, give him a small treat of some kind. Throw the treat to the back of the crate and encourage the puppy to walk in on his own. When he does so, praise him and perhaps hand him another piece of the treat through the opening in the front of the crate.

Do not succumb to your puppy's complaints about being in his crate. The puppy must learn to stay there and to do so without unnecessary complaining. A quick "no" command and a tap on the

A puppy will need to eliminate often, especially after eating, drinking, playing, and sleeping.

crate will usually get the puppy to understand that theatrics will not result in liberation. (Remember, you, the pack leader, make the rules and the puppy is seeking to learn what they are.)

Do understand that a puppy of 8 to 12 weeks will not be able to contain himself for long periods of time. Puppies of that age must relieve themselves every few hours except at night. Your schedule must be adjusted accordingly. Make sure that your puppy has relieved

A crate, such as the Nylabone® Fold-Away Pet Carrier, will keep your puppy safe and out of trouble when you can't be there to supervise him.

himself, both bowel and bladder, the last thing at night and do not dawdle when you wake up in the morning.

Your first priority in the morning is to get the puppy outdoors. Just how early this ritual will take place will depend on your puppy than much more than on you. If your Bichon is like most others, there will be no doubt in your mind when he needs to be let out. You will also learn very quickly to tell the difference between the "this is an emergency" complaint and the "I just want out" grumbling. Do not test the young puppy's ability to contain himself. His vocal demands to be let out is confirmation that the housebreaking lesson is being learned.

Should you find it necessary to be away from home all day, you will not be able to leave your puppy in a crate. However, do not make the mistake of allowing him to roam the house or even a large room at will. Confine the puppy to a very small room or partitioned-off area and cover the floor with newspaper. Make this area large enough so that the puppy will not have to relieve himself next to his bed, food bowl, or water bowl. You will soon find that the puppy will be inclined to use one particular spot to perform his bowel and bladder functions. When you are home, you must take the puppy to this exact spot to eliminate at the appropriate time.

BASIC TRAINING

Your emotional state and the environment in which you train are just as important to your dog's training as is his own state of mind at the time. Never begin training when you are irritated, distressed, or preoccupied. You should not begin basic training in a place that interferes with you or your dog's concentration. Once the commands are understood and learned, you can begin testing your dog in public places. At first, however, the two of you should work in a place where you can concentrate fully on each other.

You must stay aware of your Bichon's sensitivity level and his desire to please. Never resort to shaking or striking your Bichon puppy. A very stern "no" is usually more than sufficient and, even with the most persistent unwanted behavior, striking the ground with a rolled-up newspaper is about as extreme as you will ever need to be.

The "No" Command

There is no doubt whatsoever that one of the most important commands your Bichon puppy will ever learn is the "no" command. It is critical that the puppy learns this command just as soon as possible. One important piece of advice in using this and all other commands—*never give a command you are not prepared and able to enforce!* A good leader does not enforce rules arbitrarily. The only way a puppy learns to obey commands is to realize that once issued, commands must be complied with. Learning the "no" command should start on the first day of the puppy's arrival to your home.

Leash Training

Begin leash training by putting a soft light collar on your puppy. After a few hours of occasional scratching at the unfamiliar addition, your puppy will quickly forget that it is even there.

It may not be necessary for the puppy or adult Bichon to wear his collar and identification tags within the confines of your home, but no Bichon should ever leave home without a collar and without the attached leash held securely in your hand.

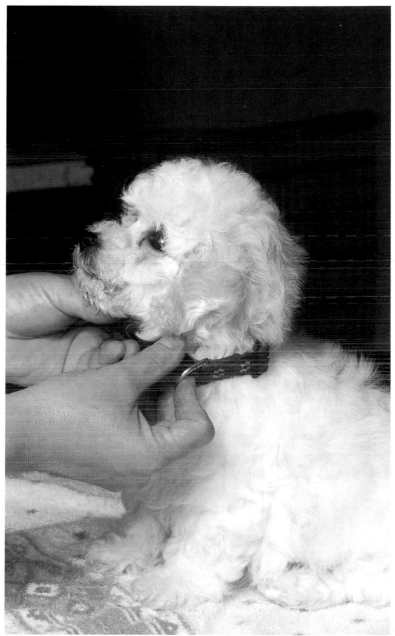

Before you start leash training, get your puppy accustomed to his collar by putting it on him and letting him wear it around the house for a few minutes at a time.

Begin getting your puppy accustomed to his collar by leaving it on for a few minutes at a time. Gradually extend the time you leave the collar on. Once this is accomplished, attach a lightweight leash to the collar while you are playing with the puppy. Do not try to guide the puppy at first. You are only trying to get the puppy used to having something attached to his collar.

Get your puppy to follow you as you move around by coaxing him along with a treat of some kind. Let the puppy smell what you have in your hand and then move a few steps back, holding the treat in front of the puppy's nose. Just as soon as the puppy takes a few steps toward you, praise him enthusiastically and continue to do so as you keep moving along.

Make the first few lessons brief and fun for the puppy. Continue the lessons in your home or yard until the puppy is completely nonchalant about the fact that he is on a leash. With a treat in one hand and the leash in the other, you can begin to use both to guide the puppy in the direction you wish to go. Eventually the two of you can venture out on the sidewalk in front of your house, and then on to adventures everywhere! This is one lesson no puppy is too young to learn.

Responding to the word "come" is one of the most important commands your Bichon will learn.

The "Come" Command

The next most important lesson for the Bichon puppy to learn is to come when called. Therefore, it is very important that the puppy learns his name as soon as possible. Constant repetition is what does the trick in teaching a puppy his name. Use the name every time you talk to your puppy.

Learning to "come" on command could save your Bichon's life when the two of you venture out into the world. "Come" is the command that a dog must understand has to be obeyed without question. However, the dog should not associate that command with fear. Your dog's response to his name and to the word "come"

Treats can be used in the initial stages of training, but your Bichon should not expect a treat every time he obeys.

should always be associated with a pleasant experience such as great praise and petting or even a food treat.

Again, remember that it is much easier to avoid the establishment of bad habits than it is to correct them once learned. *Never* give the "come" command unless you are sure your puppy will come to you. The very young puppy is far more inclined to respond to learning the "come" command than the older dog. Young puppies are entirely dependent upon you. An older dog may lose some of that dependency and become preoccupied with his surroundings. Start training your Bichon to come on command as early as possible.

Use the command initially when the puppy is already on his way to you or give the command while walking or running away from the youngster. Clap your hands and sound very happy and excited about having the puppy join in on this "game."

The very young Bichon puppy will normally want to stay as close to his owner as possible, especially in strange surroundings. When your puppy sees you moving away, his natural inclination will be to get close to you. This is a perfect time to use the "come" command.

You may want to attach a long leash or rope to the puppy's collar to ensure the correct response. Do not chase or punish your puppy for not obeying the "come" command. Doing so in the initial stages of training makes the youngster associate the command with fear, and this will result in avoidance rather than in the immediate positive response you desire. It is imperative that you praise your Bichon puppy and give him a treat when he does come to you, even if he voluntarily delays responding for many minutes.

The "Sit" and "Stay" Commands

Just as important to your Bichon's safety as the "no" command and learning to come when called are the "sit" and "stay" commands. Even very young Bichons can learn the "sit" command quickly, especially if it appears to be a game and a food treat is involved.

First, remember that the Bichon-in-training should always be on collar and leash for all of his lessons. A Bichon puppy is curious about everything that goes on around him and a puppy is not beyond getting up and walking away when he has decided that he needs to investigate something.

Give the "sit" command just before you reach down and exert pressure on your puppy's rear. Praise the puppy profusely when he does sit, even though it was you who exerted the effort. A food treat of some kind always seems to make the experience that more enjoyable for the puppy.

Continue holding the dog's rear end down and repeat the "sit" command several times. If your puppy makes an attempt to get up, repeat the command yet again while exerting pressure on his rear end until the correct position is assumed. Make your puppy stay in this position a little bit longer with each succeeding lesson. Begin with a few seconds and increase the time as lessons progress over the following weeks.

Should your puppy attempt to get up or to lie down, he should be corrected by simply saying "sit" in a firm voice. This should be accompanied by returning the dog to the desired position. Only when *you* decide that your dog should get up should he be allowed to do so. Do not test the young Bichon puppy's patience to the limits. Remember that you are dealing with a baby and the attention span of any youngster is relatively limited. When you do decide that the dog can get up, call his name, say "OK," and make a big fuss over him. Praise and a food treat are in order every time your Bichon responds correctly.

Once your puppy has mastered the "sit," you may start on the "stay" command. With your Bichon on leash and facing you, command him to "sit," then take a step or two back. If your dog attempts to get up to follow you, firmly say, "Sit, stay!" While you are saying this, raise your hand, palm toward the dog, and again command him to "stay."

If your dog attempts to get up, you must correct him at once, returning him to the sit position and repeating the "stay" command. Once your Bichon begins to understand what you want, you can gradually increase the distance you step back. With a long leash attached to your dog's collar, start with a few steps and gradually increase the distance to several yards. It is important that your Bichon learns that the "sit, stay" command must be obeyed no matter how far away you are. With advanced training, your Bichon can be taught that the command is to be obeyed even when you leave the room or are entirely out of sight.

As your Bichon becomes accustomed to responding to this lesson and is able to remain in the sit position for as long as you command, do not end the command by calling the dog to you. Walk back to your Bichon and say "OK." This will let your dog

These Bichons owned by Lori Kornfeld demonstrate two very basic positions: sit and down.

"Off" should be used instead of "down" to get your Bichon off of the furniture. The task becomes considerably more difficult, however, when you're dealing with a pile of puppies.

know that the command is over. When your Bichon becomes entirely dependable in this lesson, you can then call the dog to you.

The "sit, stay" command can take considerable time and patience to get across to puppies. You must not forget that their attention span will be short. Keep the "stay" part of the lesson very short until your puppy is about six months old.

The "Down" Command

Do not try and teach your Bichon puppy too many things at once. Wait until you have mastered one lesson quite well before moving on to something new.

When you feel quite confident that your Bichon puppy is comfortable with the "sit" and "stay" commands, you can start work on "down." This is the single word command for "lie down." Use the "down" command *only* when you want the dog to lie down. If you want your Bichon to get off your sofa or to stop jumping up on people, use the "off" command. Do not interchange these two commands. Doing so will only serve to confuse your dog, and evoking the right response will become next to impossible.

The "down" position is especially useful if you want your Bichon to remain in one place for a long period of time. Most dogs are far more inclined to stay put when lying down than when they are sitting or standing.

Teaching this command to your Bichon may take more time and patience than the previous lessons that the two of you have undertaken. It is believed by some animal behaviorists that assuming the "down" position somehow represents greater submissiveness.

With your Bichon sitting in front of and facing you, hold a treat in your right hand with the excess part of the leash in your left hand. Hold the treat under the dog's nose and slowly bring your hand down to the ground. Your dog will follow the treat with his head and neck. As he does, give the command "down" and exert *light* pressure on the dog's shoulders with your left hand. If your dog resists the pressure on his shoulders *do not continue pushing down,* as doing so will only create more resistance. Reach down and slide the dog's feet toward you until he is lying down.

An alternative method of getting your Bichon headed into the down position is to move around to the dog's right side and, as you draw his attention downward with your right hand, slide your left hand under the dog's front legs and gently slide them forward. You

Be patient when teaching your Bichon the "down"—the dog views this as a somewhat submissive position and may not be comfortable with it right away.

will undoubtedly have to be on your knees next to the youngster in order to do this.

As your Bichon's forelegs begin to slide out to the front, keep moving the treat along the ground, continuously repeating the word "down," until the dog's whole body is lying on the ground. Once your dog has assumed the position you desire, give him the treat and a lot of praise. Continue assisting your Bichon into the "down" position until he does so on his own. Be firm and be patient.

The "Heel" Command

In learning to heel, your Bichon will walk on your left side with his shoulder next to your leg no matter which direction you go or how quickly you turn. Teaching your Bichon to heel is critical to off-leash control and will not only make your daily walks far more enjoyable, it will make a far more tractable companion when the two of you are in crowded or confusing situations. We do not recommend ever allowing your Bichon to be off leash when you are away from home, but it is important to know that you can control your dog no matter what the circumstances are.

A lightweight, link-chain training collar is best to use for the heeling lesson, and changing to this collar indicates that what

The "heel" command is used in the show ring to gait a dog. Ch. Camelot Brassy Nickel, owned by Pam Goldman, struts his stuff with handler Cliff Steele.

If your Bichon is to be a show dog, you must practice the basic commands with him until they are polished to perfection.

you are doing is "business" and not just a casual stroll. These link chain collars provide both quick pressure around the neck and a snapping sound, both of which get a dog's attention. These collars are called "choke collars" by some people, but, rest assured, when the link-chain collar is used properly it will not choke the dog. The pet shop at which you purchase the training collar will be able to show you the proper way to put it on your dog.

As you train your Bichon puppy to walk along on the leash, you should accustom him to walking on your left side. The leash should cross your body from the dog's collar to your right hand. The excess portion of the leash will be folded into your right hand and your left hand on the leash will be used to make corrections with the leash.

A quick short jerk on the leash with your left hand will keep your Bichon from lunging side to side, pulling ahead, or lagging back. As you make a correction, give the "heel" command. Keep the leash loose when your dog maintains the proper position at your side.

A visit from a friendly Bichon can brighten anyone's day. Besita takes a break from agility to participate in another one of his favorite activities—therapy work.

If your dog begins to drift away, give the leash a sharp jerk, guide the dog back to the correct position, and give the "heel" command. Do not pull on the lead with steady pressure. What is needed is a sharp but gentle jerking motion to get your dog's attention.

TRAINING CLASSES

There are few limits to what a patient, consistent Bichon owner can teach his or her dog. Bichons are highly trainable—remember the breed's heritage. Once lessons are mastered, you will find that most Bichons will perform with an enthusiasm that makes all of the hard work well worthwhile.

For advanced obedience work beyond the basics, it is wise for the Bichon owner to consider local professional assistance. Professional trainers have had long-standing experience in avoiding the pitfalls of obedience training and can help you to avoid them as well.

Training assistance can be obtained in many ways. Classes are particularly good in that your dog is learning to obey commands in spite of all the interesting sights and smells of other dogs. The effort you expend to teach your dog to be a pleasant companion and good canine citizen pays off in years of enjoyable companionship.

VERSATILITY

There is no end to the number of activities that you and your Bichon can enjoy together. The breed is highly successful in both conformation shows and obedience trials. There are Canine Good Citizen certificates that can be earned through the American Kennel Club, and a new event called agility. The agility trials are actually "obstacle courses" for dogs and are fun for dog and owner alike. Bichon owners find that their dogs are particularly well suited for these events.

Owners who are not inclined toward competitive events might find enjoyment in having their Bichons serve as therapy dogs. Dogs used in this capacity are trained to assist the sick, the elderly, and often the handicapped. Other therapy dogs make visits to hospitals and homes for the aged. It has been proven that these visits provide great therapeutic value to patients.

The well-trained Bichon can provide a whole world of activities for the owner. You are limited only by the amount of time you wish to invest in this remarkable breed.

SPORT of Purebred Dogs

Welcome to the exciting and sometimes frustrating sport of dogs. No doubt you are trying to learn more about dogs or you wouldn't be deep into this book. This section covers the basics that may entice you, further your knowledge and help you to understand the dog world. If you decide to give showing, obedience or any other dog activities a try, then I suggest you seek further help from the appropriate source.

Dog showing has been a very popular sport for a long time and has been taken quite seriously by some. Others only enjoy it as a hobby.

The Kennel Club in England was formed in 1859, the American Kennel Club was established in 1884 and the Canadian Kennel Club was formed in 1888. The purpose of these clubs was to register purebred dogs and maintain their Stud Books. In the beginning, the concept of registering dogs was not readily accepted. More than 36 million dogs have been enrolled in the AKC Stud Book since its inception in 1888. Presently the kennel clubs not only register dogs but adopt and enforce rules and regulations governing dog shows, obedience trials and field trials. Over the years they have fostered and encouraged interest in the health and welfare of the purebred dog. They routinely donate funds to veterinary research for study on genetic disorders.

Following are the addresses of the kennel clubs in the United States, Great Britain and Canada.

The American Kennel Club
260 Madison Avenue
New York, NY 10010
or 5580 Centerview Drive,
Raleigh, NC 27606

The Kennel Club
1 Clarges Street
Picadilly, London, WIY 8AB, England

The Canadian Kennel Club
89 Skyway Avenue
Suite 100
Etobicoke, Ontario Canada M9W 6R4

Today there are numerous activities that are enjoyable for both the dog and the handler. Some of the activities include conformation showing, obedience competition, tracking, agility, the Canine Good Citizen Certificate, and a wide range of instinct tests that vary from breed to breed. Where you start depends upon your goals which early on may not be readily apparent.

To the victor go the spoils...Ch. Chaminade Le Blanc Chamour poses proudly with just a few of his many trophies and ribbons.

PUPPY KINDERGARTEN

Every puppy will benefit from this class. PKT is the foundation for all future dog activities from conformation to "couch potatoes." Pet owners should make an effort to attend even if they never expect to show their dog. The class is designed for puppies about three months of age with graduation at approximately five months of age. All the puppies will be in the same age group and, even though some may be a little unruly, there should not be any real problem. This class will teach the puppy some beginning obedience. As in all obedience classes the owner learns how to train his own dog. The PKT class gives the puppy the opportunity to interact with other puppies in the same age group and exposes him to strangers, which is very important. Some dogs grow up with behavior problems, one of them being fear of strangers. As you can see, there can be much to gain from this class.

A famous Scandinavian Bichon. This is Finnish/Denmark Ch. Jitterbop Cradle of Love, bred and owned by J. Kauppinen Otti of Helsinki, Finland.

Ch. Beau Monde the Firecracker, owned by Sherry Fry, became the top producing female in the breed.

CONFORMATION

Conformation showing is our oldest dog show sport. This type of showing is based on the dog's appearance— that is his structure, movement and attitude. When considering this type of showing, you need to be aware of your breed's standard and be able to evaluate your dog compared to that standard. The breeder of your puppy or other experienced breeders would be good sources for such an evaluation. Puppies can go through lots of changes over a period of time. I always say most puppies start out as promising hopefuls and then after maturing may be disappointing as show candidates. Even so this should not deter them from being excellent pets.

Usually conformation training classes are offered by the local kennel or obedience clubs. These are excellent places for training puppies. The puppy should be able to walk on a lead before entering such a class. Proper ring procedure and technique for posing (stacking) the dog will be demonstrated as well as gaiting the dog. Usually certain patterns are used in the ring such as the triangle or the "L." Conformation class, like the PKT class, will give your youngster the opportunity to socialize with different breeds of dogs and humans too.

It takes some time to learn the routine of conformation showing. Usually one starts at the puppy matches which may be AKC

Sanctioned or Fun Matches. These matches are generally for puppies from two or three months to a year old, and there may be classes for the adult over the age of 12 months. Similar to point shows, the classes are divided by sex and after completion of the classes in that breed or variety, the class winners compete for Best of Breed or Variety. The winner goes on to compete in the Group and the Group winners compete for Best in Match. No championship points are awarded for match wins.

A few matches can be great training for puppies even though there is no intention to go on showing. Matches enable the puppy to meet new people and be handled by a stranger—the judge. It is also a change of environment, which broadens the horizon for both dog and handler. Matches and other dog activities boost the confidence of the handler and especially the younger handlers.

Earning an AKC championship is built on a point system, which is different from Great Britain. To become an AKC Champion of Record the dog must earn 15 points. The number of points earned each time depends upon the number of dogs in competition. The number of points available at each show depends upon the breed, its sex and the location of the show. The United States is divided into ten AKC zones. Each zone has its own set of points. The purpose of the zones is to try to equalize the points available from breed to breed and area to area. The AKC adjusts the point scale annually.

The number of points that can be won at a show are between one and five. Three-, four- and five-point wins are considered majors. Not only does the dog need 15 points won under three different judges, but those points must include two majors under two different judges. Canada also works on a point system but majors are not required.

Dogs always show before bitches. The classes available to those seeking points are: Puppy (which may be divided into 6 to 9 months and 9 to 12 months); 12 to 18 months; Novice; Bred-by-Exhibitor; American-bred; and Open. The class winners of the same sex of each breed or variety compete against each other for Winners Dog and Winners Bitch. A Reserve Winners Dog and Reserve Winners Bitch are also awarded but do not carry any points unless the Winners win is disallowed by AKC. The Winners Dog and Bitch compete with the specials (those dogs that have attained championship) for Best of Breed or Variety, Best of Winners and

One of the authors' early champions, Ch. Drewlaine Beau Monde Deja Vu.

Best of Opposite Sex. It is possible to pick up an extra point or even a major if the points are higher for the defeated winner than those of Best of Winners. The latter would get the higher total from the defeated winner.

At an all-breed show, each Best of Breed or Variety winner will go on to his respective Group and then the Group winners will compete against each other for Best in Show. There are seven Groups: Sporting, Hounds, Working, Terriers, Toys, Non-Sporting and Herding. Obviously there are no Groups at specialty shows (those shows that have only one breed or a show such as the American Spaniel Club's Flushing Spaniel Show, which is for all flushing spaniel breeds).

Earning a championship in England is somewhat different since they do not have a point system. Challenge Certificates are awarded if the judge feels the dog is deserving regardless of the number of dogs in competition. A dog must earn three Challenge Certificates under three different judges, with at least one of these Certificates being won after the age of 12 months. Competition is very strong and entries may be higher than they are in the U.S. The Kennel Club's Challenge Certificates are only available at Championship Shows.

In England, The Kennel Club regulations require that certain dogs, Border Collies and Gundog breeds, qualify in a working capacity (i.e., obedience or field trials) before becoming a full Champion. If they do not qualify in the working aspect, then they are designated a Show Champion, which is equivalent to the AKC's Champion of Record. A Gundog may be granted the title of Field Trial Champion (FT Ch.) if it passes all the tests in the field but would also have to qualify in conformation before becoming a full Champion. A Border Collie that earns the title of Obedience Champion (Ob Ch.) must also qualify in the conformation ring before becoming a Champion.

The U.S. doesn't have a designation full Champion but does award for Dual and Triple Champions. The Dual Champion must be a Champion of Record, and either Champion Tracker, Herding Champion, Obedience Trial Champion or Field Champion. Any dog that has been awarded the titles of Champion of Record, and any two of the following: Champion Tracker, Herding Champion, Obedience Trial Champion or Field Champion, may be designated as a Triple Champion.

The shows in England seem to put more emphasis on breeder judges than those in the U.S. There is much competition within the breeds. Therefore the quality of the individual breeds should be very good. In the United States we tend to have more "all around judges" (those that judge multiple breeds) and use the breeder

The Westminster Kennel Club dog show is the most prestigious in the United States. It is held at Madison Square Garden in New York City annually.

judges at the specialty shows. Breeder judges are more familiar with their own breed since they are actively breeding that breed or did so at one time. Americans emphasize Group and Best in Show wins and promote them accordingly.

In conformation showing, handlers gait their dogs around the ring so that the judge can evaluate the dogs' movement.

It is my understanding that the shows in England can be very large and extend over several days, with the Groups being scheduled on different days. I believe there is only one all-breed show in the U.S. that extends over two days, the Westminster Kennel Club Show. In our country we have cluster shows, where several different clubs will use the same show site over consecutive days.

Westminster Kennel Club is our most prestigious show although the entry is limited to 2500. In recent years, entry has been limited to Champions. This show is more formal than the majority of the shows with the judges wearing formal attire and the handlers fashionably dressed. In most instances the quality of the dogs is superb. After all, it is a show of Champions. It is a good show to study the AKC registered breeds and is by far the most exciting—especially since it is televised! WKC is one of the few shows in this country that is still benched. This means the dog must be in his benched area during the show hours except when he is being groomed, in the ring, or being exercised.

Typically, the handlers are very particular about their appearances. They are careful not to wear something that will detract from their dog but will perhaps enhance it. American ring procedure is quite formal compared to that of other countries. I remember being reprimanded by a judge because I made a suggestion to a friend holding my second dog outside the ring. I certainly could have used more discretion so I would not call attention to myself. There is a certain etiquette expected between the judge and exhibitor and among the other exhibitors. Of course it is not always the case but the judge is supposed to be polite, not engaging in small talk or even acknowledging that he knows the handler. I understand that there is a more informal and relaxed atmosphere at the shows in other countries. For instance, the dress code is more casual. I can see where this might be more fun for the exhibitor and especially for the novice. This country is very handler-oriented in many of the breeds. It is true, in most instances, that the experienced professional handler can present the dog better and will have a feel for what a judge likes.

In England, Crufts is The Kennel Club's own show and is most assuredly the largest dog show in the world. They've been known to have an entry of nearly 20,000, and the show lasts four days. Entry is only gained by qualifying through winning in specified classes at another Championship Show. Westminster is strictly conformation, but Crufts exhibitors and spectators enjoy not only conformation but obedience, agility and a multitude of exhibitions as well. Obedience was admitted in 1957 and agility in 1983.

If you are handling your own dog, please give some consideration to your apparel. For sure the dress code at matches is more informal than the point shows. However, you should wear something a little more appropriate than beach attire or ragged jeans and bare feet. If you check out the handlers and see what is presently fashionable, you'll catch on. Men usually dress with a shirt and tie and a nice sports coat. Whether you are male or female, you will want to wear comfortable clothes and shoes. You need to be able to run with your dog and you certainly don't want to take a chance of falling and hurting yourself. Heaven forbid, if nothing else, you'll upset your dog. Women usually wear a dress or two-piece outfit, preferably with pockets to carry bait, comb, brush, etc. In this case men are the lucky ones with all their pockets. Ladies, think about where your dress will be if you need to kneel on the floor and also think about running. Does it allow freedom to do so?

Years ago, after toting around all the baby paraphernalia, I found toting the dog and necessities a breeze. You need to take along dog; crate; ex pen (if you use one); extra newspaper; water pail and water; all required grooming equipment, including hair dryer and extension cord; table; chair for you; bait for dog and lunch for you and friends; and, last but not least, clean up materials, such as plastic bags, paper towels, and perhaps a bath towel and some shampoo—just in case. Don't forget your entry confirmation and directions to the show.

Junior Showmanship is a great way for young people to learn and practice handling skills. The handlers are judged solely on their ability, not on their dogs' conformation.

If you are showing in obedience, then you will want to wear pants. Many of our top obedience handlers wear pants that are color-coordinated with their dogs. The philosophy is that imperfections in the black dog will be less obvious next to your black pants.

Whether you are showing in conformation, Junior Showmanship or obedience, you need to watch the clock and be sure you are not late. It is customary to pick up your conformation armband a few minutes before the start of the class. They will not wait for you and if you are on the show grounds and not in the ring, you will upset everyone. It's a little more complicated picking up your obedience armband if you show later in the class. If you have not picked up your armband and they get to your number, you may not be allowed to show. It's best to pick up your armband early, but then you may show earlier than expected if other handlers don't pick up. Customarily all conflicts should be discussed with the judge prior to the start of the class.

Junior Showmanship

The Junior Showmanship Class is a wonderful way to build self confidence even if there are no aspirations of staying with the dog-show game later in life. Frequently, Junior Showmanship becomes the background of those who become successful exhibitors/handlers in the future. In some instances it is taken very seriously, and success is measured in terms of wins. The Junior Handler is judged solely on his ability and skill in presenting his dog. The dog's conformation is not to be considered by the

You'll need to bring your grooming equipment with you to the show to make sure that your Bichon looks his best in the ring.

Ch. Sea Star's Another Valentino checks out the action at a show from his vantage point on the grooming table.

judge. Even so the condition and grooming of the dog may be a reflection upon the handler.

Usually the matches and point shows include different classes. The Junior Handler's dog may be entered in a breed or obedience class and even shown by another person in that class. Junior Showmanship classes are usually divided by age and perhaps sex. The age is determined by the handler's age on the day of the show. The classes are:

Novice Junior for those at least ten and under 14 years of age who at time of entry closing have not won three first places in a Novice Class at a licensed or member show.

Novice Senior for those at least 14 and under 18 years of age who at the time of entry closing have not won three first places in a Novice Class at a licensed or member show.

Open Junior for those at least ten and under 14 years of age who at the time of entry closing have won at least three first places in a Novice Junior Showmanship Class at a licensed or member show with competition present.

Open Senior for those at least 14 and under 18 years of age who at time of entry closing have won at least three first places in a Novice Junior Showmanship Class at a licensed or member show with competition present.

Junior Handlers must include their AKC Junior Handler number on each show entry. This needs to be obtained from the AKC.

CANINE GOOD CITIZEN

The AKC sponsors a program to encourage dog owners to train their dogs. Local clubs perform the pass/fail tests, and dogs who pass are awarded a Canine Good Citizen Certificate. Proof of vaccination is required at the time of participation. The test includes:

1. Accepting a friendly stranger.
2. Sitting politely for petting.
3. Appearance and grooming.
4. Walking on a loose leash.
5. Walking through a crowd.
6. Sit and down on command/staying in place.
7. Come when called.
8. Reaction to another dog.
9. Reactions to distractions.
10. Supervised separation.

If more effort was made by pet owners to accomplish these exercises, fewer dogs would be cast off to the humane shelter.

OBEDIENCE

Obedience is necessary, without a doubt, but it can also become a wonderful hobby or even an obsession. In my opinion, obedience classes and competition can provide wonderful companionship, not only with your dog but with your classmates or fellow competitors. It is always gratifying to discuss your dog's problems with others who have had similar experiences. The AKC acknowledged Obedience around 1936, and it has changed tremendously even though many of the exercises are basically the same. Today, obedience competition is just that—very competitive. Even so, it is possible for every obedience exhibitor to come home a winner (by earning qualifying scores) even though he/she may not earn a placement in the class.

Most of the obedience titles are awarded after earning three qualifying scores (legs) in the appropriate class under three different judges. These classes offer a perfect score of 200, which is extremely

Flying high over the broad jump! In obedience and agility events, the jumps are adjusted for different sized dogs.

rare. Each of the class exercises has its own point value. A leg is earned after receiving a score of at least 170 and at least 50 percent of the points available in each exercise. The titles are:

Companion Dog—CD
This is called the Novice Class and the exercises are:

1. Heel on leash and figure 8	40 points
2. Stand for examination	30 points
3. Heel free	40 points
4. Recall	30 points
5. Long sit—one minute	30 points
6. Long down—three minutes	30 points
Maximum total score	200 points

Companion Dog Excellent—CDX
This is the Open Class and the exercises are:

1. Heel off leash and figure 8	40 points
2. Drop on recall	30 points
3. Retrieve on flat	20 points
4. Retrieve over high jump	30 points
5. Broad jump	20 points
6. Long sit—three minutes (out of sight)	30 points
7. Long down—five minutes (out of sight)	30 points
Maximum total score	200 points

Utility Dog—UD

The Utility Class exercises are:

1. Signal Exercise	40 points
2. Scent discrimination-Article 1	30 points
3. Scent discrimination-Article 2	30 points
4. Directed retrieve	30 points
5. Moving stand and examination	30 points
6. Directed jumping	40 points
Maximum total score	200 points

After achieving the UD title, you may feel inclined to go after the UDX and/or OTCh. The UDX (Utility Dog Excellent) title went into effect in January 1994. It is not easily attained. The title requires qualifying simultaneously ten times in Open B and Utility B but not necessarily at consecutive shows.

The OTCh (Obedience Trial Champion) is awarded after the dog has earned his UD and then goes on to earn 100 championship points, a first place in Utility, a first place in Open and another first place in either class. The placements must be won under three different judges at all-breed obedience trials. The points are determined by the number of dogs competing in the Open B and Utility B classes. The OTCh title precedes the dog's name.

Obedience matches (AKC Sanctioned, Fun, and Show and Go) are usually available. Usually they are sponsored by the local obedience clubs. When preparing an obedience dog for a title, you will find matches very helpful. Fun Matches and Show and Go Matches are more lenient in allowing you to make corrections in the ring. I frequently train (correct) in the ring and inform the judge that I would like to do so and to please mark me "exhibition." This means that I will not be eligible for any prize. This type of training is

Besita easily clears a training jump. This talented performer has earned the CDX title in obedience competition.

Agility is just as much work for the handler as it is for the dog—and just as much fun! Handlers run through the course with their dogs to direct them and give commands.

usually very necessary for the Open and Utility Classes. AKC Sanctioned Obedience Matches do not allow corrections in the ring since they must abide by the AKC Obedience Regulations. If you are interested in showing in obedience, then you should contact the AKC for a copy of the Obedience Regulations.

TRACKING

Tracking is officially classified obedience, but I feel it should have its own category. There are three tracking titles available: Tracking Dog (TD), Tracking Dog Excellent (TDX), Variable Surface Tracking (VST). If all three tracking titles are obtained, then the dog officially becomes a CT (Champion Tracker). The CT will go in front of the dog's name.

A TD may be earned anytime and does not have to follow the other obedience titles. There are many exhibitors that prefer tracking to obedience, and there are others like myself that do both. In my experience with small dogs, I prefer to earn the CD and CDX before attempting tracking. My reasoning is that small dogs are closer to the mat in the obedience rings and therefore it's too easy to put the nose down and sniff. Tracking encourages sniffing. Of course this depends on the dog. I've had some dogs that tracked around the ring and others (TDXs) who wouldn't think of sniffing in the ring.

AGILITY

Agility was first introduced by John Varley in England at the Crufts Dog Show, February 1978, but Peter Meanwell, competitor and judge, actually developed the idea. It was officially recognized in the early '80s. Agility is extremely popular in England and Canada and growing in popularity in the U.S. The AKC acknowledged agility in August 1994. Dogs must be at least 12 months of age to be entered. It is a fascinating sport that the dog, handler and spectators enjoy to the utmost. Agility is a spectator sport! The dog performs off lead. The handler either runs with his dog or positions himself on the course and directs his dog with verbal and hand signals over a timed course over or through a variety of obstacles including a time out or pause. One of the main drawbacks to agility is finding a place to train. The obstacles take up a lot of space and it is very time consuming to put up and take down courses.

The titles earned at AKC agility trials are Novice Agility Dog (NAD), Open Agility Dog (OAD), Agility Dog Excellent (ADX), and Master Agility Excellent (MAX). In order to acquire an agility title, a dog must earn a qualifying score in its respective class on

Jake, owned by Gail Huston, goes through a tire jump on the agility course. He has earned several agility and obedience titles.

three separate occasions under two different judges. The MAX will be awarded after earning ten qualifying scores in the Agility Excellent Class.

GENERAL INFORMATION

Obedience, tracking and agility allow the purebred dog with an *Jake is at it again...this time up and over the A-frame obstacle. Notice his handler giving encouragement on the side.*

Indefinite Listing Privilege (ILP) number or a limited registration to be exhibited and earn titles. Application must be made to the AKC for an ILP number.

The American Kennel Club publishes a monthly *Events* magazine that is part of the *Gazette*, their official journal for the sport of purebred dogs. The *Events* section lists upcoming shows and the secretary or superintendent for them. The majority of the conformation shows in the U.S. are overseen by licensed superintendents. Generally the entry closing date is approximately two-and-a-half weeks before the actual show. Point shows are fairly expensive, while the match shows cost about one third of the point show entry fee. Match shows usually take entries the day of the show but some are pre-entry. The best way to find match show information is through your local kennel club. Upon asking, the AKC can provide you with a list of superintendents, and you can write and ask to be put on their mailing lists.

Obedience trial and tracking test information is available through the AKC. Frequently these events are not superintended, but put on by the host club. Therefore you would make the entry with the event's secretary.

As you have read, there are numerous activities you can share with your dog. Regardless what you do, it does take teamwork. Your dog can only benefit from your attention and training. I hope this chapter has enlightened you and hope, if nothing else, you will attend a show here and there. Perhaps you will start with a puppy kindergarten class, and who knows where it may lead!

HEALTH CARE

Veterinary medicine has become far more sophisticated than what was available to our ancestors. This can be attributed to the increase in household pets and consequently the demand for better care for them. Also human medicine has become far more complex. Today diagnostic testing in veterinary medicine parallels human diagnostics. Because of better technology we can expect our pets to live healthier lives thereby increasing their life spans.

THE FIRST CHECK UP

You will want to take your new puppy/dog in for its first check up within 48 to 72 hours after acquiring it. Many breeders strongly recommend this check up and so do the humane shelters. A puppy/dog can appear healthy but it may have a serious problem that is not apparent to the layman. Most pets have some type of a minor flaw that may never cause a real problem.

Unfortunately if he/she should have a serious problem, you will want to consider the consequences of keeping the pet and the attachments that will be formed, which may be broken prematurely. Keep in mind there are many healthy dogs looking for good homes.

This first check up is a good time to establish yourself with the veterinarian and learn the office policy regarding their hours and how they handle emergencies. Usually the breeder or another conscientious pet owner is a good reference for locating a capable veterinarian. You should be aware that not all veterinarians give the same quality of service. Please do not make your selection on the least expensive clinic, as they may be short changing your pet. There is the possibility that eventually it will cost you more due to improper diagnosis, treatment, etc. If you are selecting a new veterinarian, feel free to ask for a tour of the clinic. You should inquire about making an appointment for a tour since all clinics are working clinics, and therefore may not be available all day for sightseers. You may worry less if you see where your pet will be spending the day if he ever needs to be hospitalized.

Your puppy depends on you for health care. Find a good veterinarian and keep up a regular routine of preventive care and maintenance.

THE PHYSICAL EXAM

Your veterinarian will check your pet's overall condition, which includes listening to the heart; checking the respiration; feeling the abdomen, muscles and joints; checking the mouth, which includes the gum color and signs of gum disease along with plaque buildup; checking the ears for signs of an infection or ear mites; examining the eyes; and, last but not least, checking the condition of the skin and coat.

He should ask you questions regarding your pet's eating and elimination habits and invite you to relay your questions. It is a good idea to prepare a list so as not to forget anything. He should discuss the proper diet and the quantity to be fed. If this should differ from your breeder's recommendation, then you should convey to him the breeder's choice and see if he approves. If he recommends changing the diet, then this should be done over a few days so as not to cause a gastrointestinal upset. It is customary to take in a fresh stool sample (just a small amount) for a test for intestinal parasites. It must be fresh, preferably within 12 hours, since the eggs hatch quickly and after hatching will not be observed under the microscope. If your pet isn't obliging then, usually the technician can take one in the clinic.

IMMUNIZATIONS

It is important that you take your puppy/dog's vaccination

record with you on your first visit. In case of a puppy, presumably the breeder has seen to the vaccinations up to the time you acquired custody. Veterinarians differ in their vaccination protocol. It is not unusual for your puppy to have received vaccinations for distemper, hepatitis, leptospirosis, parvovirus and parainfluenza every two to three weeks from the age of five or six weeks. Usually this is a combined injection and is typically called the DHLPP. The DHLPP is given through at least 12 to 14 weeks of age, and it is customary to continue with another parvovirus vaccine at 16 to 18 weeks. You may wonder why so many immunizations are necessary. No one knows for sure when the puppy's maternal antibodies are gone, although it is customarily accepted that distemper antibodies are gone by 12 weeks. Usually parvovirus antibodies are gone by 16 to 18 weeks of age. However, it is possible for the maternal antibodies to be gone at a much earlier age or even a later age. Therefore immunizations are started at an early age. The vaccine will not give immunity as long as there are maternal antibodies.

Once a puppy's maternal antibodies are gone, it is important to make sure he receives the proper vaccinations. Your veterinarian will set up a schedule for your Bichon.

The rabies vaccination is given at three or six months of age depending on your local laws. A vaccine for bordetella (kennel cough) is advisable and can be given anytime from the age of five weeks. The coronavirus is not commonly given unless there is a problem locally. The Lyme vaccine is necessary in endemic areas. Lyme disease has been reported in 47 states.

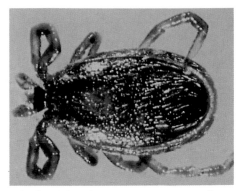

The deer tick is the most common carrier of Lyme disease. Photo courtesy of Virbac Laboratories, Inc., Fort Worth, Texas.

Distemper

This is virtually an incurable disease. If the dog recovers, he is subject to severe nervous disorders. The virus attacks every tissue in the body and resembles a bad cold with a fever. It can cause a runny nose and eyes and cause gastrointestinal disorders, including a poor appetite, vomiting and diarrhea. The virus is carried by raccoons, foxes, wolves, mink and other dogs. Unvaccinated youngsters and senior citizens are very susceptible. This is still a common disease.

Hepatitis

This is a virus that is most serious in very young dogs. It is spread by contact with an infected animal or its stool or urine. The virus affects the liver and kidneys and is characterized by high fever, depression and lack of appetite. Recovered animals may be afflicted with chronic illnesses.

Leptospirosis

This is a bacterial disease transmitted by contact with the urine of an infected dog, rat or other wildlife. It produces severe symptoms of fever, depression, jaundice and internal bleeding and was fatal before the vaccine was developed. Recovered dogs can be carriers, and the disease can be transmitted from dogs to humans.

Parvovirus

This was first noted in the late 1970s and is still a fatal disease. However, with proper vaccinations, early diagnosis and prompt treatment, it is a manageable disease. It attacks the bone marrow and intestinal tract. The symptoms include depression, loss of appetite, vomiting, diarrhea and collapse. Immediate medical attention is of the essence.

Rabies

This is shed in the saliva and is carried by raccoons, skunks, foxes, other dogs and cats. It attacks nerve tissue, resulting in paralysis and death. Rabies can be transmitted to people and is virtually always fatal. This disease is reappearing in the suburbs.

Bordetella (Kennel Cough)

The symptoms are coughing, sneezing, hacking and retching accompanied by nasal discharge usually lasting from a few days to several weeks. There are several disease-producing organisms responsible for this disease. The present vaccines are helpful but do not protect for all the strains. It usually is not life threatening but in some instances it can progress to a serious bronchopneumonia. The disease is highly contagious. The vaccination should be given routinely for dogs that come in contact with other dogs, such as through boarding, training class or visits to the groomer.

Coronavirus

This is usually self limiting and not life threatening. It was first noted in the late '70s about a year before parvovirus. The virus produces a yellow/brown stool and there may be depression, vomiting and diarrhea.

Lyme Disease

This was first diagnosed in the United States in 1976 in Lyme, CT in people who lived in close proximity to the deer tick. Symptoms may include acute lameness, fever, swelling of joints and loss of appetite. Your veterinarian can advise you if you live in an endemic area.

After your puppy has completed his puppy vaccinations, you will continue to booster the DHLPP once a year. It is customary to booster the rabies one year after the first vaccine and then, depending on where you live, it should be boostered every year or every three years. This depends on your local laws. The Lyme and corona vaccines are boostered annually and it is recommended that the bordetella be boostered every six to eight months.

ANNUAL VISIT

I would like to impress the importance of the annual check up, which would include the booster vaccinations, check for intestinal parasites and test for heartworm. Today in our very busy world it is rush, rush and see "how much you can get for how little." Unbelievably, some non-veterinary businesses have entered into the vaccination business. More harm than good can come to your dog through improper vaccinations, possibly from inferior vaccines and/or the wrong schedule. More than likely you truly care about your companion dog and over the years you have devoted much time and expense to his well being. Perhaps you are unaware that a vaccination is not just a vaccination. There is more involved. Please, please follow through with regular physical examinations. It is so important for your veterinarian to know your dog and this is especially true during middle age through the geriatric years. More than likely your older dog will require more than one physical a year. The annual physical is good preventive medicine. Through early diagnosis

Young puppies are especially vulnerable to disease. Vaccinations are an absolute necessity, as some serious illnesses can be passed from dog to dog.

and subsequent treatment your dog can maintain a longer and better quality of life.

INTESTINAL PARASITES

Hookworms

These are almost microscopic intestinal worms that can cause anemia and therefore serious problems, including death, in young puppies. Hookworms can be transmitted to humans through penetration of the skin. Puppies may be born with them.

Roundworms

These are spaghetti-like worms that can cause a potbellied appearance and dull coat along with more severe symptoms, such as vomiting, diarrhea and coughing. Puppies acquire these while in the mother's uterus and through lactation. Both hookworms and roundworms may be acquired through ingestion.

Whipworms

These have a three-month life cycle and are not acquired through the dam. They cause intermittent diarrhea usually with mucus. Whipworms are possibly the most difficult worm to eradicate. Their eggs are very resistant to most environmental factors and can last for years until the proper conditions enable them to mature. Whipworms are seldom seen in the stool.

Intestinal parasites are more prevalent in some areas than others.

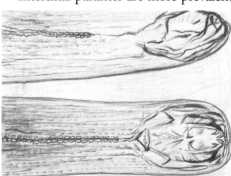

Hookworms are almost microscopic intestinal worms that can cause anemia and therefore serious problems, even death.

Climate, soil and contamination are big factors contributing to the incidence of intestinal parasites. Eggs are passed in the stool, lay on the ground and then become infective in a certain number of days. Each of the above worms has a different life cycle. Your best chance of becoming and remaining worm-free

Worms can be passed from mother to pup, so be sure to have your puppy checked for parasites by your veterinarian.

is to always pooper-scoop your yard. A fenced-in yard keeps stray dogs out, which is certainly helpful.

I would recommend having a fecal examination on your dog twice a year or more often if there is a problem. If your dog has a positive fecal sample, then he will be given the appropriate medication and you will be asked to bring back another stool sample in a certain period of time (depending on the type of worm) and then be rewormed. This process goes on until he has at least two negative samples. The different types of worms require different medications. You will be wasting your money and doing your dog an injustice by buying over-the-counter medication without first consulting your veterinarian.

OTHER INTERNAL PARASITES

Coccidiosis and Giardiasis

These protozoal infections usually affect puppies, especially in places where large numbers of puppies are brought together. Older dogs may harbor these infections but do not show signs unless they are stressed. Symptoms include diarrhea, weight loss and lack of appetite. These infections are not always apparent in the fecal examination.

Diet plays a large role in your Bichon's health. Although it may be tempting to share "people food," especially when he looks at you with that pleading stare, don't give in!

Tapeworms

Seldom apparent on fecal floatation, they are diagnosed frequently as rice-like segments around the dog's anus and the base of the tail. Tapeworms are long, flat and ribbon like, sometimes several feet in length, and made up of many segments about five-eighths of an inch long. The two most common types of tapeworms found in the dog are:

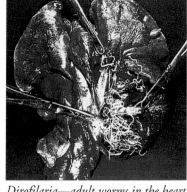

Dirofilaria—adult worms in the heart of a dog. Courtesy of Merck AgVet.

(1) First the larval form of the flea tapeworm parasite must mature in an intermediate host, the flea, before it can become infective. Your dog acquires this by ingesting the flea through licking and chewing.

(2) Rabbits, rodents and certain large game animals serve as intermediate hosts for other species of tapeworms. If your dog should eat one of these infected hosts, then he can acquire tapeworms.

HEARTWORM DISEASE

This is a worm that resides in the heart and adjacent blood vessels of the lung that produces microfilaria, which circulate in the bloodstream. It is possible for a dog to be infected with any number of worms from one to a hundred that can be 6 to 14 inches long. It is a life-threatening disease, expensive to treat and easily prevented. Depending on where you live, your veterinarian may recommend a preventive year-round and either an annual or semiannual blood test. The most common preventive is given once a month.

EXTERNAL PARASITES

Fleas

These pests are not only the dog's worst enemy but also enemy to the owner's pocketbook. Preventing is less expensive than treating, but regardless I think we'd prefer to spend our money elsewhere. I would guess that the majority of our dogs are allergic to the bite of a flea, and in many cases it only takes one flea bite. The protein in the flea's saliva is the culprit. Allergic dogs have a reaction, which usually results in a "hot spot." More than likely such a reaction will involve a trip to the veterinarian for treatment. Yes, prevention is less expensive. Fortunately today there are several good products available.

If there is a flea infestation, no one product is going to correct the problem. Not only will the dog require treatment so will the environment. In general flea collars are not very effective although there is now available an "egg" collar that will kill the eggs on the dog. Dips are the most economical but they are messy. There are some effective shampoos and treatments available through pet shops and veterinarians. An oral tablet arrived on the American market in 1995 and was popular in Europe the previous year. It sterilizes the female flea but will not kill adult fleas. Therefore the tablet, which is given monthly, will decrease the flea population but is not a "cure-all." Those dogs that suffer from flea-bite allergy will still be subjected to the bite of the flea. Another popular parasiticide is permethrin, which is applied to the back of the dog in one or two places depending on the dog's weight. This product works as a repellent causing the flea to get "hot feet" and jump off. Do not confuse this product with some of the organophosphates that are also applied to the dog's back.

To prevent and eliminate flea infestation in the house, use a safe insecticide to kill adult fleas and an insect growth regulator to stop eggs and larvae in the environment.

Some products are not usable on young puppies. Treating fleas should be done under your veterinarian's guidance. Frequently it is necessary to combine products and the layman does not have the knowledge regarding possible toxicities. It is hard to believe but there are a few dogs that do have a natural resistance to fleas. Nevertheless it would be wise to treat all pets at the same time. Don't forget your cats. Cats just love to prowl the neighborhood and consequently return with unwanted guests.

The cat flea is the most common flea of both dogs and cats. Courtesy of Fleabusters, Rx for Fleas, Inc., Fort Lauderdale, Florida.

Adult fleas live on the dog but their eggs drop off the dog into the environment. There they go through four larval stages before reaching adulthood, and thereby are able to jump back on the poor unsuspecting dog. The cycle resumes and takes between 21 to 28 days under ideal conditions. There are environmental products available that will kill both the adult fleas and the larvae.

Ticks

Ticks carry Rocky Mountain Spotted Fever, Lyme disease and can cause tick paralysis. They should be removed with tweezers, trying to pull out the head. The jaws carry disease. There is a tick

Dogs love to romp in the grass...and ticks love dogs. The Bichon's ample coat makes a great hiding place for ticks, so be sure to check him carefully after he plays outside.

A puppy can't take care of himself—he depends on his owners to make sure that he grows up healthy and strong.

preventive collar that does an excellent job. The ticks automatically back out on those dogs wearing collars.

Sarcoptic Mange
This is a mite that is difficult to find on skin scrapings. The pinnal reflex is a good indicator of this disease. Rub the ends of the pinna (ear) together and the dog will start scratching with his foot. Sarcoptes are highly contagious to other dogs and to humans although they do not live long on humans. They cause intense itching.

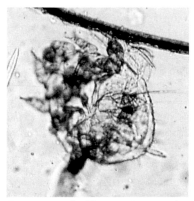

Sarcoptes are highly contagious to other dogs and to humans, although they do not live long on humans. They cause intense itching.

Demodectic Mange
This is a mite that is passed from the dam to her puppies. It affects youngsters age three to ten months. Diagnosis is confirmed by skin scraping. Small areas of alopecia around the eyes, lips and/or forelegs become visible. There is little itching unless there is a secondary bacterial infection. Some breeds are afflicted more than others.

Cheyletiella
This causes intense itching and is diagnosed by skin scraping. It lives in the outer layers of the skin of dogs, cats, rabbits and humans. Yellow-gray scales may be found on the back and the rump, top of the head and the nose.

To Breed or Not To Breed
More than likely your breeder has requested that you have your puppy neutered or spayed. Your breeder's request is based on what is healthiest for your dog and what is most beneficial for your breed. Experienced and conscientious breeders devote many years into developing a bloodline. In order to do this, he makes every effort to plan each breeding in regard to conformation, temperament and health. This type of breeder

does his best to perform the necessary testing (i.e., OFA, CERF, testing for inherited blood disorders, thyroid, etc.). Testing is expensive and sometimes very disheartening when a favorite dog doesn't pass his health tests. The health history pertains not only to the breeding stock but to the immediate ancestors. Reputable breeders do not want their offspring to be bred indiscriminately. Therefore you may be asked to neuter or spay your puppy. Of course there is always the exception, and your breeder may agree to let you breed your dog under his direct supervision. This is an important concept. More and more effort is being made to breed healthier dogs.

Spay/Neuter

There are numerous benefits of performing this surgery at six months of age. Unspayed females are subject to mammary and ovarian cancer. In order to prevent mammary cancer she must be spayed prior to her first heat cycle. Later in life, an unspayed female may develop a pyometra (an infected uterus), which is definitely life threatening.

Spaying is performed under a general anesthetic and is easy on the young dog. As you might expect it is a little harder on the older dog, but that is no reason to deny her the surgery. The surgery removes the ovaries and uterus. It is important to remove all the ovarian tissue. If some is left behind, she could remain attractive to males. In order to view the ovaries, a reasonably long incision is necessary. An ovariohysterectomy is considered major surgery.

Neutering the male at a young age will inhibit some characteristic male behavior that owners frown upon. I have found my boys will not hike their legs and mark territory if they are neutered at six months of age. Also neutering at a young age has hormonal benefits, lessening the chance of hormonal aggressiveness.

Surgery involves removing the testicles but leaving the scrotum. If there should be a retained testicle, then he definitely needs to be neutered before the age of two or three years. Retained testicles can develop into cancer. Unneutered males are at risk for testicular cancer, perineal fistulas, perianal tumors and fistulas and prostatic disease.

Intact males and females are prone to housebreaking accidents. Females urinate frequently before, during and after heat cycles, and

If, after careful consideration, you decide to breed your Bichon, talk to as many experienced breeders as possible and gather all the information you can.

males tend to mark territory if there is a female in heat. Males may show the same behavior if there is a visiting dog or guests.

Surgery involves a sterile operating procedure equivalent to human surgery. The incision site is shaved, surgically scrubbed and draped. The veterinarian wears a sterile surgical gown, cap, mask and gloves. Anesthesia should be monitored by a registered technician. It is customary for the veterinarian to recommend a pre-anesthetic blood screening, looking for metabolic problems and a ECG rhythm strip to check for normal heart function. Today anesthetics are equal to human anesthetics, which enables your dog to walk out of the clinic the same day as surgery.

Some folks worry about their dog gaining weight after being neutered or spayed. This is usually not the case. It is true that some dogs may be less active so they could develop a problem, but my own dogs are just as active as they were before surgery. I have a hard time keeping weight on them. However, if your dog should begin to gain, then you need to decrease his food and see to it that he gets a little more exercise.

DENTAL CARE for Your Dog's Life

So you've got a new puppy! You also have a new set of puppy teeth in your household. Anyone who has ever raised a puppy is abundantly aware of these new teeth. Your puppy will chew anything he can reach, chase your shoelaces, and play "tear the rag" with any piece of clothing he can find. When puppies are newly born, they have no teeth. At about four weeks of age, puppies of most breeds begin to develop their deciduous or baby teeth. They begin eating semi-solid food, fighting and biting with their littermates, and learning discipline from their mother. As their new teeth come in, they inflict more pain on their mother's breasts, so her feeding sessions become less frequent and shorter. By the time pups are six or eight weeks of age, the mother will start growling to warn her pups when they are fighting too roughly or hurting her as they nurse too much with their new teeth.

Puppies need to chew. It is a necessary part of their physical and mental development. They develop muscles and necessary life skills as they drag objects around, fight over possession, and vocalize alerts and warnings. Puppies chew on things to explore

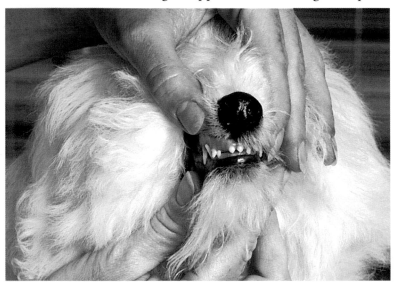

Each time your Bichon has a physical exam, the veterinarian should thoroughly inspect his lips, teeth, and gums.

The appropriate toys and bones are excellent tools to relieve your Bichon's need to chew and keep his teeth and jaw occupied.

Aside from veterinary examinations, checking your Bichon's mouth on a weekly basis for sores, foreign objects, teeth problems, etc. will help maintain good oral health.

their world. They are using their sense of taste to determine what is food and what is not. How else can they tell an electrical cord from a lizard? At about four months of age, most puppies begin shedding their baby teeth. Often these teeth need some help to come out and make way for the permanent teeth. The incisors (front teeth) will be replaced first. Then, the adult canine or fang teeth erupt. When the baby tooth is not shed before the permanent tooth comes in, veterinarians call it a retained deciduous tooth. This condition will often cause gum infections by trapping hair and debris between the permanent tooth and the retained baby tooth. Puppies that have adequate chew toys will have less destructive behavior, develop more physically, and have less chance of retained deciduous teeth.

During the first year, your dog should be seen by your veterinarian at regular intervals. Your veterinarian will let you know when to bring in your puppy for vaccinations and parasite examinations. At each visit, your veterinarian should inspect the lips, teeth, and mouth as part of a complete physical examination.

You should take some part in the maintenance of your dog's oral health by examining your dog's mouth weekly throughout his first year to make sure there are no sores, foreign objects, tooth problems, etc. If your dog drools excessively, shakes his head, or has bad breath, consult your veterinarian. By the time your dog is six months old, the permanent teeth are all in and plaque can start to accumulate on the tooth surfaces. This is when your dog needs to develop good dental care habits to prevent calculus buildup on his teeth. Brushing is best. That is a fact that cannot be denied. However, some dogs do not like their teeth brushed regularly, or you may not be able to accomplish the

All dogs need safe chew toys to keep their teeth and jaws occupied.

task. In that case, you should consider a product that will help prevent plaque and calculus buildup.

By the time dogs are four years old, 75 percent of them have periodontal disease. It is the most common infection in dogs. Yearly examinations by your veterinarian are essential to maintaining your dog's good health. If your veterinarian detects periodontal disease, he or she may recommend a prophylactic cleaning. To do a thorough cleaning, it will be necessary to put your dog under anesthesia. With modern gas anesthetics and monitoring equipment, the procedure is pretty safe. Your veterinarian will scale the teeth with an ultrasound scaler or hand instrument. This removes the calculus from the teeth. If there are calculus deposits below the gum line, the veterinarian will plane the roots to make them smooth. After all of the calculus has been removed, the teeth are polished with pumice in a polishing cup. If any medical or surgical treatment is needed, it is done at this time. The final step would be fluoride treatment and your follow-up treatment at home. If the periodontal disease is advanced, the veterinarian may prescribe a medicated mouth rinse or antibiotics for use at home. Make sure your dog has safe, clean and attractive chew toys and treats.

As your dog ages, professional examination and cleaning should become more frequent. The mouth should be inspected at least once a year. Your veterinarian may recommend visits every six months. In the geriatric patient, organs such as the heart, liver, and kidneys do not function as well as when they were young. Your veterinarian will

Your Bichon's oral care is just as important as his grooming or nutritional needs. Developing good oral habits from the beginning of your puppy's life will keep his teeth healthy.

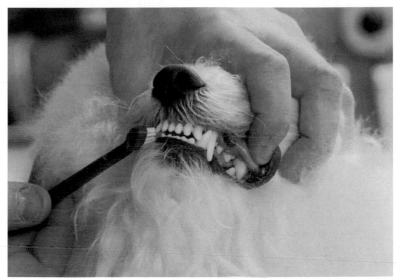

Check your Bichon Frise's teeth and mouth as part of his regular grooming routine.

probably want to test these organs' functions prior to using general anesthesia for dental cleaning. If your dog is a good chewer and you work closely with your veterinarian, your dog can keep all of his teeth all of his life. However, as your dog ages, his sense of smell, sight, and taste will diminish. He may not have the desire to chase, trap, or chew his toys. He will also not have the energy to chew for long periods, as arthritis and periodontal disease make chewing painful. This will leave you with more responsibility for keeping his teeth clean and healthy. The dog that would not let you brush his teeth at one year of age may let you brush his teeth now that he is ten years old.

If you train your dog to have good chewing habits as a puppy, he will have healthier teeth throughout his life.

TRAVELING with Your Dog

The earlier you start traveling with your new puppy or dog, the better. He needs to become accustomed to traveling. However, some dogs are nervous riders and become carsick easily. It is helpful if he starts with an empty stomach. Do not despair, as it will go better if you continue taking him with you on short fun rides. How would you feel if every time you rode in the car you stopped at the doctor's for an injection? You would soon dread that nasty car. Older dogs that tend to get carsick may have more of a problem adjusting to traveling. Those dogs that are having a serious problem may benefit from some medication prescribed by the veterinarian.

Do give your dog a chance to relieve himself before getting into the car. It is a good idea to be prepared for a cleanup with a leash, paper towels, bag, and terry cloth towel.

The safest place for your dog is in a fiberglass crate, although close confinement can promote carsickness in some dogs. If your dog is nervous you can try letting him ride on the seat next to you or in someone's lap.

An alternative to the crate would be to use a car harness made for dogs and/or a safety strap attached to the harness or collar. Whatever

The Bichon is a companion dog—he will be happy to accompany you whenever you go.

Give your dog plenty of toys to keep him occupied in the car.

you do, do not let your dog ride in the back of a pickup truck unless he is securely tied on a very short lead. I've seen trucks stop quickly and, even though the dogs are tied, they have fallen out and been dragged.

I do occasionally let my dogs ride loose with me because I really enjoy their companionship, but in all honesty they are safer in their crates. I have a friend whose van rolled in an accident but his dogs, in their fiberglass crates, were not injured nor did they escape. Another advantage of the crate is that it is a safe place to leave your dog if you need to run into the store, and remember to leave the windows open. Keep in mind that while many dogs are overly protective in their crates, this may not be enough to deter dognappers. In some states it is against the law to leave a dog in the car unattended.

Never leave a dog loose in the car wearing a collar and leash. I have known more than one dog that has killed himself by hanging. Do not let him put his head out an open window. Foreign debris can be blown into his eyes. When leaving your dog unattended in a car, consider the temperature. It can take less than five minutes to reach temperatures over 100 degrees Fahrenheit.

TRIPS

Perhaps you are taking a trip. Give consideration to what is best for your dog—traveling with you or boarding. When traveling by car, van, or motor home, you need to think ahead about locking your vehicle. In all probability you have many valuables in the car and do not wish to leave it unlocked. Perhaps most valuable and not replaceable is your dog. Give thought to securing your vehicle and providing adequate ventilation for him. Another consideration for you when traveling with your dog is medical problems that may arise and little inconveniences, such as exposure to external parasites. Some areas of the country are quite flea infested. You may want to carry flea spray with you. This is even a good idea when staying in motels. Quite possibly you are not the only occupant of the room.

Unbelievably, many motels and even hotels do allow canine guests, even some very first-class ones. Gaines Pet Foods Corporation publishes *Touring With Towser*, a directory of domestic hotels and motels that accommodate guests with dogs. Their address is Gaines TWT, PO Box 5700, Kankakee, IL, 60902. I would recommend that you call ahead to any motel you may be considering and see if they accept pets. Sometimes it is necessary to pay a deposit against room damage. Of course you are more likely to gain accommodations for a small dog than a large dog. Also the management feels reassured when you mention that your dog will be crated. Because my dogs tend to bark when I leave the room, I leave the TV on nearly full blast to deaden the noises outside that tend to encourage my dogs to bark. If you do travel with your dog, take along plenty of baggies so that you can clean up after him. When we all do our share in cleaning up, we make it possible for motels to continue accepting our pets. As a matter of fact, you should practice cleaning up everywhere you take your dog.

Depending on where your are traveling, you may need an up-to-date health certificate issued by your veterinarian. It is good policy to take along your dog's medical information, which would include the name, address, and phone number of your veterinarian, vaccination record, rabies certificate, and any medication he is taking.

AIR TRAVEL

When traveling by air, you need to contact the airlines to check their policy. Usually you have to make arrangements up to a couple of weeks in advance for traveling with your dog. The airlines require your dog to travel in an airline-approved fiberglass crate. Usually these can be purchased through the airlines but they are also readily available in most pet-supply stores. If your dog is not accustomed to a crate, then it is a good idea to get him acclimated to it before your trip. The day of the actual trip you should withhold water about 1 hour ahead of departure and no food for about 12 hours. The airlines generally have temperature restrictions, which do not allow pets to travel if it is either too cold or too hot. Frequently these restrictions are based on the temperatures at the departure and arrival airports. It's best to inquire about a health certificate, which usually needs to be issued within ten days of departure. You should arrange for non-stop, direct flights and if a commuter plane should be involved, check to see if it will carry dogs. Some don't. The Humane Society of the United States has put together a tip sheet for airline traveling. You can receive a copy by sending a self-addressed stamped envelope to the following address:

The Humane Society of the United States
Tip Sheet
2100 L Street NW
Washington, DC 20037.

Regulations differ for traveling outside of the country and are sometimes changed without notice. Well in advance you need to write or call the appropriate consulate or agricultural department

Dogs that participate in dog shows will have to become accustomed to extensive travel.

for instructions. Some countries have lengthy quarantines (six months), and countries differ in their rabies vaccination requirements. For instance, it may have to be given at least 30 days ahead of your departure.

Do make sure your dog is wearing proper identification. You never know when you might be in an accident and separated from your dog, or your dog could be frightened and somehow manage to escape and run away. When I travel, my dogs wear collars with engraved nameplates with my name, phone number, and city.

Another suggestion would be to carry in-case-of-emergency instructions. These would include the address and phone number of a relative or friend, your veterinarian's name, address and phone number, and your dog's medical information.

BOARDING KENNELS

Perhaps you have decided that you need to board your dog. Your veterinarian can recommend a good boarding facility or possibly a pet sitter that will come to your house. It is customary for the boarding kennel to ask for proof of vaccination for the DHLPP, rabies and bordetella vaccine. The bordetella should have been given within six months of boarding. This is for your protection. If they do not ask for this proof I would not board at their kennel. Ask

A reputable boarding kennel will require that dogs receive the vaccination for kennel cough no less than two weeks before their scheduled stay.

Before embarking on a long trip, decide what is best for your Bichon. He may be more comfortable staying at home with a pet sitter or in a reputable boarding kennel.

about flea control. Those dogs that suffer flea-bite allergy can get in trouble at a boarding kennel. Unfortunately boarding kennels are limited on how much they are able to do.

For more information on pet sitting, contact NAPPS:
National Association of Professional Pet Sitters
1200 G Street, NW
Suite 760
Washington, DC 20005.

Our clinic has technicians that pet sit and technicians that board clinic patients in their homes. This may be an alternative for you. Ask your veterinarian if they have an employee that can help you. There is a definite advantage of having a technician care for your dog, especially if your dog is on medication or is a senior citizen.

You can write for a copy of *Traveling With Your Pet* from ASPCA, Education Department, 441 E. 92nd Street, New York, NY 10128.

IDENTIFICATION and Finding the Lost Dog

There are several ways of identifying your dog. The old standby is a collar with dog license, rabies, and ID tags. Unfortunately collars have a way of being separated from the dog and tags fall off. I am not suggesting you shouldn't use a collar and tags. If they stay intact and on the dog, they are the quickest way of identification.

For several years, owners have been tattooing their dogs. Some tattoos use a number with a registry. Here lies the problem because there are several registries to check. If you wish to tattoo, use your social security number. The humane shelters have the means to trace it. It is usually done on the inside of the rear thigh. The area is first shaved and numbed. There is no pain, although a few dogs do not like the buzzing sound. Occasionally, tattooing is not legible and needs to be redone.

The newest method of identification is microchipping. The microchip is a computer chip that is no larger than a grain of rice. The veterinarian implants it by injection between the shoulder blades. The dog feels no discomfort. If your dog is lost and picked up by the humane society, they can trace you by

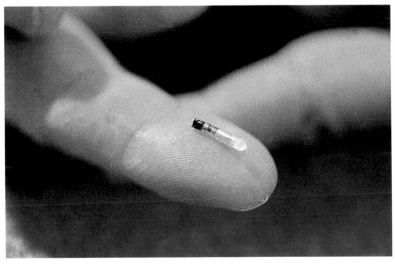

The newest method of identification is microchipping. The microchip is a computer chip that is no bigger than a grain of rice.

scanning the microchip, which has its own code. Microchip scanners are friendly to other brands of microchips and their registries. The microchip comes with a dog tag saying the dog is microchipped. It is the safest way of identifying your dog.

FINDING THE LOST DOG

I am sure you will agree with me that there would be little worse than losing your dog. Responsible pet owners rarely lose their dogs. They do not let their dogs run free because they don't want harm to come to them. Not only that but in most, if not all, states there is a leash law.

Beware of fenced-in yards. They can be a hazard. Dogs find ways to escape either over or under the fence. Another fast exit is through the gate that perhaps the neighbor's child left unlocked.

Below is a list that hopefully will be of help to you if you need it. Remember don't give up, keep looking. Your dog is worth your efforts.

1. Contact your neighbors and put flyers with a photo on it in their mailboxes. Information you should include would be the dog's name, breed, sex, color, age, source of identification, when your dog was last seen and where, and your name and phone numbers. It may be helpful to say the dog needs medical care. Offer a *reward*.

2. Check all local shelters daily. It is also possible for your dog to be picked up away from home and end up in an out-of-the-way shelter. Check these too. Go in person. It is not good enough to call. Most shelters are limited on the time they can hold dogs then they are put up for adoption or euthanized. There is the possibility that your dog will not make it to the shelter for several days. Your dog could have been wandering or someone may have tried to keep him.

3. Notify all local veterinarians. Call and send flyers.

4. Call your breeder. Frequently breeders are contacted when one of their breed is found.

5. Contact the rescue group for your breed.

6. Contact local schools—children may have seen your dog.

7. Post flyers at the schools, groceries, gas stations, convenience stores, veterinary clinics, groomers and any other place that will allow them.

8. Advertise in the newspaper.

9. Advertise on the radio.

BEHAVIOR and Canine Communication

Studies of the human/animal bond point out the importance of the unique relationships that exist between people and their pets. Those of us who share our lives with pets understand the special part they play through companionship, service and protection. For many, the pet/owner bond goes beyond simple companionship; pets are often considered members of the family. A leading pet food manufacturer recently conducted a nationwide survey of pet owners to gauge just how important pets were in their lives. Here's what they found:

- 76 percent allow their pets to sleep on their beds
- 78 percent think of their pets as their children
- 84 percent display photos of their pets, mostly in their homes.
- 100 percent talk to their pets
- 97 percent think that their pets understand what they're saying
  Are you surprised?

Senior citizens show more concern for their own eating habits when they have the responsibility of feeding a dog. Seeing that the dog is routinely exercised encourages the owner to think of schedules that otherwise may seem unimportant to the senior citizen. The older owner may be arthritic and feeling poorly but with responsibility for his dog he has a reason to get up and get moving. It is a big plus if his dog is an attention seeker that will demand such from his owner.

A Bichon from "down under." Keleb Majestic Image was born in the USA but now lives in Australia with owners Frank Vallely and Rudy Van Voorst.

Portrait of a champion...Ch. Sea Star's Beau Brummel, by artist Ed Glazbrook.

Over the last couple of decades, it has been shown that pets relieve the stress of those who lead busy lives. Owning a pet has been known to lessen the occurrence of heart attack and stroke.

Many single folks thrive on the companionship of a dog. Lifestyles are very different from a long time ago, and today more individuals seek the single life. However, they receive fulfillment from owning a dog.

Most likely the majority of our dogs live in family environments. The companionship they provide is well worth the effort involved. In my opinion, every child should have the opportunity to have a family dog. Dogs teach responsibility through understanding their care, feelings, and even respecting their life cycles. Frequently those children who have not been exposed to dogs grow up afraid of dogs, which isn't good. Dogs sense timidity and some will take advantage of the situation.

Today more dogs are serving as service dogs. Since the origination of the Seeing Eye dogs years ago, we now have trained hearing dogs. Also dogs are trained to provide service for the handicapped and are

Look at the smiling faces on this family of Bichons! It's easy to see why this breed is so popular as a show dog, therapy dog, and all-around family dog.

able to perform many different tasks for their owners. Search and Rescue dogs, with their handlers, are sent throughout the world to assist in recovery of disaster victims. They are life savers.

Therapy dogs are very popular with nursing homes, and some hospitals even allow them to visit. The inhabitants truly look forward to their visits. I have taken a couple of my dogs visiting and left in tears when I saw the response of the patients. They wanted and were allowed to have my dogs in their beds to hold and love.

Nationally there is a Pet Awareness Week to educate students and others about the value and basic care of our pets. Many countries take an even greater interest in their pets than Americans do. In those countries the pets are allowed to accompany their owners into restaurants and shops, etc. In the US this freedom is only available to our service dogs. Even so we think very highly of the human/animal bond.

CANINE BEHAVIOR

Canine behavior problems are the number-one reason for pet owners to dispose of their dogs, either through new homes, humane shelters, or euthanasia. Unfortunately there are too many owners who are unwilling to devote the necessary time to properly train their dogs. On the other hand, there are those who not only are concerned about inherited health problems but are also aware of the dog's mental stability.

You may realize that a breed and his group relatives (i.e., sporting, hounds, etc.) show tendencies to behavioral characteristics. An experienced breeder can acquaint you with his breed's personality. Unfortunately many breeds are labeled with poor temperaments when actually the breed as a whole is not affected but only a small percentage of individuals within the breed.

If the breed in question is very popular, then of course there may be a higher number of unstable dogs. Do not label a breed good or bad. I know of absolutely awful-tempered dogs within one of our most popular, lovable breeds.

Inheritance and environment contribute to the dog's behavior. Some naïve people suggest inbreeding as the cause of bad temperaments. Inbreeding only results in poor behavior if the ancestors carry the trait. If there are excellent temperaments behind

Since behavioral traits are shared by breed members and passed on to each generation, only the dogs with the most stable temperaments should be bred.

the dogs, then inbreeding will promote good temperaments in the offspring. Did you ever consider that inbreeding is what sets the characteristics of a breed? A purebred dog is the end result of inbreeding. This does not spare the mixed-breed dog from the same problems. Mixed-breed dogs frequently are the offspring of purebred dogs.

When planning a breeding, I like to observe the potential stud and his offspring in the show ring. If I see unruly behavior, I try to look into it further. I want to know if it is genetic or environmental, due to the lack of training and socialization. A good breeder will avoid breeding mentally unsound dogs.

Not too many decades ago most of our dogs led a different lifestyle than what is prevalent today. Usually mom stayed home so the dog had human companionship and someone to discipline him if needed. Not much was expected from the dog. Today's mom works and everyone's life is at a much faster pace.

The dog may have to adjust to being a "weekend" dog. The family is gone all day during the week, and the dog is left to his own devices for entertainment. Some dogs sleep all day waiting for their family to come home and others become wigwam wreckers if given the opportunity. Crates do ensure the safety of the dog and the house. However, he could become physically and emotionally

All dogs need lots of love, attention, and interaction with their human families.

Bichon puppy or retriever in disguise? An indoor game of fetch can help your young friend run off some of his puppy exuberance.

crippled if he doesn't get enough exercise and attention. We still appreciate and want the companionship of our dogs although we expect more from them. In many cases we tend to forget dogs are just that—*dogs* and not human beings.

When it is necessary to crate dogs for long periods of time, try to make time for them in the evenings and on the weekends. Also, we try to do something together before I leave for work. Maybe it helps them to have the companionship of other dogs. They accept their crates as their personal "houses" and seem to be content with their routine and thrive on trying their best to please me.

SOCIALIZING AND TRAINING

Many prospective puppy buyers lack experience regarding the proper socialization and training needed to develop the type of pet we all desire. In the first 18 months, training does take some work. Trust me, it is easier to start proper training before there is a problem that needs to be corrected.

The initial work begins with the breeder. The breeder should start socializing the puppy at five to six weeks of age and cannot let up. Human socializing is critical up through 12 weeks of age and likewise important during the following months. The litter should be left together during the first few weeks but it is necessary to separate them by ten weeks of age. Leaving them together after that time will increase competition for litter dominance. If puppies are not socialized with people by 12 weeks of age, they will be timid in later life.

The eight- to ten-week age period is a fearful time for puppies. They need to be handled very gently around children and adults. There should be no harsh discipline during this time. Starting at 14 weeks of age, the puppy begins the juvenile period, which ends when he reaches sexual maturity around 6 to 14 months of age. During the juvenile period he needs to be introduced to strangers (adults, children, and other dogs) on the home property. At sexual maturity he will begin to bark at strangers and become more protective. Males start to lift their legs to urinate but if you desire you can inhibit this behavior by walking your boy on leash away from trees, shrubs, fences, etc.

Perhaps you are thinking about an older puppy. You need to inquire about the puppy's social experience. If he has lived in a kennel, he may have a hard time adjusting to people and environmental stimuli. Assuming he has had a good social upbringing, there are advantages to an older puppy.

Training includes puppy kindergarten and a minimum of one to two basic training classes. During these classes you will learn how

Interacting with their littermates gives puppies a sense of pack order. The dominant one in the litter always manages to stay "on top" of things.

to dominate your youngster. This is especially important if you own a large breed of dog. It is somewhat harder, if not nearly impossible, for some owners to be the Alpha figure when their dog towers over them. You will be taught how to properly restrain your dog. This concept is important. Again it puts you in the Alpha

Crouching down to put yourself closer to the puppy's level and encouraging the puppy to take treats are two ways to help a fearful pup feel more at ease.

position. All dogs need to be restrained many times during their lives. Believe it or not, some of our worst offenders are the eight-week-old puppies that are brought to our clinic. They need to be gently restrained for a nail trim, but the way they carry on you would think we were killing them. In comparison, their vaccination is a "piece of cake." When we ask dogs to do something that is not agreeable to them, then their worst comes out. Life will be easier for your dog if you expose him at a young age to the necessities of life—proper behavior and restraint.

UNDERSTANDING THE DOG'S LANGUAGE

Most authorities agree that the dog is a descendent of the wolf. The dog and wolf have similar traits. For instance both are pack oriented and prefer not to be isolated for long periods of time. Another characteristic is that the dog, like the wolf, looks to the leader—Alpha—for direction. Both the wolf and the dog communicate through body language, not only within their pack but with outsiders.

Every pack has an Alpha figure. The dog looks to you, or should look to you, to be that leader. If your dog doesn't receive the proper training and guidance, he very well may replace you as Alpha. This would be a serious problem and is certainly a disservice to your dog.

Eye contact is one way the Alpha wolf keeps order within his pack. You are Alpha so you must establish eye contact with your puppy. Obviously your puppy will have to look at you. Practice eye contact even if you need to hold his head for five to ten seconds at a time. You can give him a treat as a reward. Make sure your eye contact is gentle and not threatening. Later, if he has been naughty, it is permissible to give him a long, penetrating look. I caution you there are some older dogs that never learned eye contact as puppies and cannot accept eye contact. You should avoid eye contact with these dogs since they feel threatened and will retaliate as such.

BODY LANGUAGE

The play bow, when the forequarters are down and the hindquarters are elevated, is an invitation to play. Puppies play fight, which helps them learn the acceptable limits of biting. This is necessary for later in their lives. Nevertheless, an owner may be falsely reassured by the playful nature of his dog's aggression. Playful aggression toward another dog or human may be an indication of serious aggression in the future. Owners should never play fight or play tug-of-war with any dog that is inclined to be dominant.

Signs of submission are as follows:

1. Avoids eye contact.
2. Active submission—the dog crouches down, ears back and the tail is lowered.
3. Passive submission—the dog rolls on his side with his hindlegs in the air and frequently urinates.

Signs of dominance are:

1. Makes eye contact.
2. Stands with ears up, tail up and the hair raised on his neck.
3. Shows dominance over another dog by standing at right angles over it.

Dominant dogs tend to behave in characteristic ways such as:

1. The dog may be unwilling to move from his place (i.e., reluctant to give up the sofa if the owner wants to sit there).
2. He may not part with toys or objects in his mouth and may show possessiveness with his food bowl.
3. He may not respond quickly to commands.
4. He may be disagreeable for grooming and dislikes to be petted.

Dogs are popular because of their sociable nature. Those that have contact with humans during the first 12 weeks of life regard them as a member of their own species—their pack. All dogs have the potential for both dominant and submissive behavior. Only through experience and training do they learn to whom it is appropriate to show which behavior. Not all dogs are concerned with dominance but owners need to be aware of that potential. It is wise for the owner to establish his dominance early on.

A human can express dominance or submission toward a dog in the following ways:

1. Meeting the dog's gaze signals dominance. Averting the gaze signals submission. If the dog growls or threatens, averting the gaze is the first avoiding action to take—it may prevent attack. It is important to establish eye contact in the puppy. The older dog that has not been exposed to eye contact may see it as a threat and will not be willing to submit.

2. Being taller than the dog signals dominance; being lower signals submission. This is why, when attempting to make friends with a strange dog or catch the runaway, one should kneel down to his level. Some owners see their dogs become dominant when allowed on the furniture or on the bed. Then he is at the owner's level.

In the winter, when the Bichon has little exposure to the sun, his black nose may fade to pink. The black returns with the arrival of warmer weather.

3. An owner can gain dominance by ignoring all the dog's social initiatives. The owner pays attention to the dog only when he obeys a command.

No dog should be allowed to achieve dominant status over any adult or child. Ways of preventing are as follows:

1. Handle the puppy gently, especially during the three- to four-month period.

2. Let the children and adults handfeed him and teach him to take food without lunging or grabbing.

3. Do not allow him to chase children or joggers.

4. Do not allow him to jump on people or mount their legs. Even females may be inclined to mount. It is not only a male habit.

5. Do not allow him to growl for any reason.

6. Don't participate in wrestling or tug-of-war games.

7. Don't physically punish puppies for aggressive behavior. Restrain him from repeating the infraction and teach an alternative behavior. Dogs should earn everything they receive from their owners. This would include sitting to receive petting or treats, sitting before going out the door and sitting to receive the collar and leash. These types of exercises reinforce the owner's dominance.

Young children should never be left alone with a dog. It is important that children learn some basic obedience commands so they have some control over the dog. They will gain the respect of their dog.

Fear is a common problem in dogs; in fact, it can make some Bichons want to hide!

It's a big world out there, especially when you're as tiny as this Bichon puppy.

FEAR

One of the most common problems dogs experience is being fearful. Some dogs are more afraid than others. On the lesser side, which is sometimes humorous to watch, my dog can be afraid of a strange object. He acts silly when something is out of place in the house. I call his problem perceptive intelligence. He realizes the abnormal within his known environment. He does not react the same way in strange environments since he does not know what is normal.

On the more serious side is a fear of people. This can result in backing off, seeking his own space and saying "leave me alone" or it can result in an aggressive behavior that may lead to challenging the person. Respect that the dog wants to be left alone and give him time to come forward. If you approach the cornered dog, he may resort to snapping. If you leave him alone, he may decide to come forward, which should be rewarded with a treat. Years ago we had a dog that behaved in this manner. We coaxed people to stop by the house and make friends with our fearful dog. She learned to take the treats and after weeks of work she overcame her suspicions and made friends more readily.

Some dogs may initially be too fearful to take treats. In these cases it is helpful to make sure the dog hasn't eaten for about 24 hours. Being a little hungry encourages him to accept the treats, especially if they are of the "gourmet" variety. I have a dog that worries about strangers since people seldom stop by my house. Over the years she has learned a cue and jumps up quickly to visit anyone sitting on the sofa. She learned by herself that all guests on the sofa were to be trusted friends. I think she felt more comfortable with them being at her level, rather than towering over her.

Dogs can be afraid of numerous things, including loud noises and thunderstorms. Invariably the owner rewards (by comforting) the dog when it shows signs of fearfulness. I had a terrible problem with my favorite dog in the Utility obedience class. Not only was he intimidated in the class but he was afraid of noise and afraid of displeasing me. Frequently he would knock down the bar jump, which clattered dreadfully. I gave him credit because he continued to try to clear it, although he was terribly scared. I finally learned to "reward" him every time he knocked down the jump. I would jump up and down, clap my hands and tell him how great he was. My psychology worked, he relaxed and eventually cleared the jump with ease. When your dog is frightened, direct his attention to something else and act happy. Don't dwell on his fright.

AGGRESSION

Some different types of aggression are: predatory, defensive, dominance, possessive, protective, fear induced, noise provoked, "rage" syndrome (unprovoked aggression), maternal and aggression

Dogs can become fearful of or aggressive toward things they are not familiar with, which is why regular human contact and exposure to other dogs is necessary.

directed toward other dogs. Aggression is the most common behavioral problem encountered. Protective breeds are expected to be more aggressive than others but with the proper upbringing they can make very dependable companions. You need to be able to read your dog.

This Bichon copes with the stresses of living the glamorous life by taking a break and playing it cool.

Many factors contribute to aggression including genetics and environment. An improper environment, which may include the living conditions, lack of social life, excessive punishment, being attacked or frightened by an aggressive dog, etc., can all influence a dog's behavior. Even spoiling him and giving too much praise may be detrimental. Isolation and the lack of human contact or exposure to frequent teasing by children or adults also can ruin a good dog.

Lack of direction, fear, or confusion lead to aggression in those dogs that are so inclined. Any obedience exercise, even the sit and down, can direct the dog and overcome fear and/or confusion. Every dog should learn these commands as a youngster, and there should be periodic reinforcement.

When a dog is showing signs of aggression, you should speak calmly (no screaming or hysterics) and firmly give a command that he understands, such as the sit. As soon as your dog obeys, you have assumed your dominant position. Aggression presents a problem because there may be danger to others. Sometimes it is an emotional issue. Owners may consciously or unconsciously encourage their dog's aggression. Other owners show responsibility by accepting the problem and taking measures to keep it under control. The owner is responsible for his dog's actions, and it is not wise to take a chance on someone being bitten, especially a child. Euthanasia is the solution for some owners and in severe cases this may be the best choice. However, few dogs are that dangerous and very few are that

After a long day, this Bichon enjoys nothing more than relaxing on the couch with a good book...about his favorite breed, of course.

much of a threat to their owners. If caution is exercised and professional help is gained early on, then I surmise most cases can be controlled.

Some authorities recommend feeding a lower protein (less than 20 percent) diet. They believe this can aid in reducing aggression. If the dog loses weight, then vegetable oil can be added. Veterinarians and behaviorists are having some success with pharmacology. In many cases treatment is possible and can improve the situation.

If you have done everything according to "the book" regarding training and socializing and are still having a behavior problem, don't procrastinate. It is important that the problem gets attention before it is out of hand. It is estimated that 20 percent of a veterinarian's time may be devoted to dealing with problems before they become so intolerable that the dog is separated from its home and owner. If your veterinarian isn't able to help, he should refer you to a behaviorist.

My most important advice to you is to be aware of your dog's actions. Even so, remember dogs are dogs and will behave as such even though we might like them to be perfect little people. You and your dog will become neurotic if you worry about every little indiscretion. When there is reason for concern—don't waste time. Seek guidance. Dogs are meant to be loved and enjoyed.

References:

Manual of Canine Behavior, Valerie O'Farrell, British Small Animal Veterinary Association.

Good Owners, Great Dogs, Brian Kilcommons, Warner Books.

RESOURCES

Bichon Frise Club of America, Inc.
Corresponding Secretary: Joanne Styles
32 Oak Street
Centerreach, NY 11720
www.bichon.org

American Kennel Club
260 Madison Avenue
New York, NY 10016
or 5580 Centerview Drive
Raleigh, NC 27606
919-233-3600
919-233-9767
www.akc.org

The Kennel Club
1 Clarges Street
Picadilly, London WIY 8AB, England

Canadian Kennel Club
100-89 Skyway Avenue
Etobicoke, Ontario, Canada M9W6R4

United Kennel Club, Inc.
100 E. Kilgore Road
Kalamazoo, MI 49002-5584
616-343-9020
www.ukcdogs.com

United States Dog Agility Association (USDAA)
PO Box 850955
Richardson, TX 75085-0955
(972) 231-9700
Information Line: (888) AGILITY
Web site: http://www.usdaa.com/
Email: info@usdaa.com

INDEX